EXPLORING THE WORLD OF BIRDS

AN EQUINOX GUIDE TO AVIAN LIFE

ADRIAN FORSYTH AND LAUREL AZIZ

CAMDEN HOUSE

Canadian Cataloguing in Publication Data

Forsyth, Adrian
    Exploring the world of birds

ISBN 0-920656-98-6 (bound) ISBN 0-920656-94-3 (pbk.)

1. Birds — Behavior — Juvenile literature.
2. Birds — Habitat — Juvenile literature.
I. Aziz, Laurel Ellen. II. Title.

QL676.2.F67   1990   j598   C90-093907-9

Front Cover: Bruce Lyon

Back Cover: Jerg Kroener

Trade distribution by
Firefly Books
250 Sparks Avenue
Willowdale, Ontario
Canada M2H 2S4

Printed and bound in Canada by
D.W. Friesen & Sons Ltd.
Altona, Manitoba, for
Camden House Publishing
(a division of Telemedia Publishing Inc.)
7 Queen Victoria Road
Camden East, Ontario K0K 1J0

Designed by: Andrew McLachlan

Colour separations by
Hadwen Graphics
Ottawa, Ontario

CONTENTS

One hundred and forty million years ago, the world was still blanketed in vast, shallow swamps. Rough, shrubby vegetation and giant tree ferns sprouted from the rocky ground. Massive dinosaurs waded across rivers and swamps to fish for food, and the earth crawled with the first explosion of animals able to live on land. Around that time, the first bird, known as *Archaeopteryx*, appeared.

Our information about this bird is limited to what can be read in fossils. By studying the beautifully preserved specimens of *Archaeopteryx* discovered in limestone quarries in southern Germany, palaeontologists have determined that with its sturdy skeleton, strong legs and feet and long, bony tail, it looked much like a large, flying lizard. Its sharp teeth and tough, ragged scales were evidence of its descendancy from the reptiles, and although *Archaeopteryx* did not fly, it could glide from tree to tree using its primitive wings. In fact, *Archaeopteryx* was on its way to developing the key features that have made birds an evolutionary success: feathers and flight.

Millions of years later, the weather-resistant scales that first signalled the evolution of warm-blooded animals have evolved into a superior form of insulation – soft, fluffy feathers. Unlike reptiles, which have a variable body temperature that changes according to their surroundings, birds exploit the insulating value of feathers to stabilize a high body temperature so that they can remain active despite the cold. By harnessing this body heat, birds

This fossilized impression of feathers is the oldest of its kind and provides evidence that *Archaeopteryx* is the first known bird.

can use their warm bodies to incubate their hard-shelled eggs.

Modern birds are precision machines; they are quick, agile and coordinated. Flight has enabled them to accomplish remarkable feats. Hopping and gliding have been replaced by daringly high speeds and long-distance travel. The falcon dives toward the earth at more than 300 kilometres per hour in pursuit of prey; the golden plover migrates 40,000 kilometres every year from its breeding ground to a warm winter home. The swallow can glean dustlike clouds of insects from the sky for its food, and the tiny hummingbird can drink from the flowers of tall trees. While animals such as tropical lizards, frogs, snakes and the North American flying squirrel are passive gliders that use the wind to carry them to their destinations, many members of the bird family are able to generate enough power to lift them-

While this tiny day-old Arctic loon is able to swim, it will not hesitate to climb up onto its mother's back once its highly absorbent down feathers become saturated with cold water.

When fruit ripens in the summer, Bohemian waxwings consume it in great quantities; as a consequence, these birds have become important seed dispersers.

selves off the ground from a standing start—an advantage for capturing prey, escaping danger or positioning a nest safely.

But flight did not come without a price. While mammals perform many complicated manoeuvres with their paws, such as grasping prey and manipulating nest material, birds have lost the use of their forelimbs and are, as a result, awkward on the ground. These limitations are compensated for by other capabili-ties, however: their bills are handy for feeding and nest building, and their keen senses and quick reflexes help birds to avoid danger.

From a single ancestor, modern birds have branched out into 8,500 different species that occupy every habitat on Earth and a variety of ecological niches. Some live in the hottest deserts, while the penguin is at ease on the ice of the Antarctic. Birds hunt, scavenge, graze and fish, by day and by night, over land and ocean. There are seed-, insect- and flesh-eating birds. And they have developed some remarkable sensory abilities. Some hunt by sight and others, like the turkey vulture, by smell. Owls can hear mice scrambling along runways tunnelled beneath the snow. The South American oilbird is a night-feeding fruit-eater that lives in caves and uses sonar to find its way around in the dark. The nesting habits of birds reflect the same diversity: many nest on the ground; others work like masons, pasting their mud structures on the face of a vertical surface; and some do not build any nest at all.

After years on the wing, the compact little swift has given up many of the traits necessary for survival on the ground, while the blubbery penguin, with its supple hide and shortened, paddlelike wings, is as agile in the water as most other birds are in the air. Yet the loon can do both: it is powerful in flight and can hold its breath underwater for 200 metres when it chases a fish. The avian world begins to make sense only when we understand that the variety of shapes, sizes and behaviours birds display are choices that help each one survive in its environment.

Bird watchers outnumber all other amateur naturalists, and scientists devote more time to the study of birds than to that of any other life form. On a very basic level, humans simply enjoy the visual beauty of a peacock's plumage and the haunting sound of a loon's cry. Yet the more we watch birds, the more we find there is to discover. Birds capture our imagination, and studying them can provide us with a lifetime of pleasure and learning.

This young least bittern is already able to strike the "freeze" position necessary for avoiding danger in its marshy habitat.

What does an animal that stands three metres tall, runs like a horse and tips the scales at 160 kilograms have in common with a tiny, hovering creature the size of a bumblebee? Both are birds, and despite the differences in size and shape between the ostrich and the hummingbird, both are built from the same basic parts. In fact, each separate species is one of 8,500 versions of the same design.

All birds, and only birds, have feathers and wings. Their smoothly curved and uninterrupted body shape creates little wind resistance, and all flying birds have hollow bones and a lightweight frame with many air-filled cavities to lighten their weight; they have also disposed of most excess body tissue. Birds remain lightweight at both ends: they have no teeth and few bones in their heads, and their tails have been replaced by feathers. Their legs are usually slight and bony – the minimum required to act as landing gear.

What little weight a flying bird does carry is well balanced and centred in its chest muscles, which surround the breastbone. These are a bird's largest and strongest muscles, often representing about 25 percent of its total weight. They provide the power that drives the wings, enabling lots of oxygen to enter the bird's bloodstream; the faster a bird can flap its wings, the more energy it will have to fly.

Since all birds are warm-blooded, they have a minimum size limit. Cold-blooded creatures such as reptiles survive the cold because their

The broad-tailed hummingbird must feed constantly to produce energy but falls into a torpor at night to reduce its output.

body temperature drops with the temperature of the air; some insects hibernate through cold weather; others, like bees, build up a substance in their systems that works like antifreeze to keep them from freezing solid. But warm-blooded animals must maintain a constant body temperature. Therefore, birds eat more food during cold weather, increasing their energy production to compensate for their heat loss. The smaller the warm-blooded ani-

mal, the faster it gives off body heat, so it must eat even more food to offset the loss of energy.

But no warm-blooded animal will survive if energy is lost faster than it can be produced. The tiny hummingbirds feed all day long and are about as small as a bird can be. Only a diet of energy-rich nectar makes it possible for them to gather as much energy as they radiate and lose.

Being large also has its difficulties. It takes more flying power, bigger wings and more powerful flight muscles to generate the lift necessary to get a big bird off the ground. The largest flying birds must use both the wind and their gliderlike soaring ability to remain airborne. The heaviest birds, like ostriches and penguins, are simply unable to fly. Because they occupy habitats that are safe from most land predators, penguins and ostriches have developed unique body shapes that are compatible with a form of locomotion less demanding than flight. The ostrich has become a large, heavy, running bird that flees predators on foot, while the penguin swims like a porpoise when it is chased by an enemy.

The penguin's heavy body, well insulated with fat and covered with a dense, multilayered hide, helps it survive in the Antarctic cold. You might also guess that herons and flamingos fish by wading into shallow water on their long, spindly legs and that the muscularly built eagles and falcons are hunters. By examining a bird's body and asking yourself a few questions about the purpose of its shape and size, you can learn a lot about the bird's life.

Strolling along a desert road, a pair of ostriches remains alert. Confronted by danger, these birds, using their muscular legs and tough padded feet, can kick and run like horses.

An osprey's feet are powerful and deadly weapons. Diving out of the sky with its toes widespread, an osprey grabs a fish that has made the fatal mistake of swimming too near the surface. With razor-sharp talons that pierce the scales and swiftly kill its struggling prey, the osprey's thick, muscular feet hoist the fish from the water and carry it back to the nest.

But not many birds use their feet for hunting. The chief purpose of birds' feet is for perching. The clawed digits on a bird's foot are its toes, and the scaly leg that extends up to the first joint is the instep of the foot. Well concealed beneath the feathers is the true leg; so the jointed portion that looks like the knee is really a modified ankle. A bird, therefore, stands on its toes, not flat on its feet.

Unusually long toes give the bird's foot greater extension and flexibility when it is perching. The toes curl around and grip a tree limb, and special tendons in the thigh pull the claw closed when a bird settles its weight to keep it upright.

The woodpecker and the tree creeper use their agile feet for climbing. With two toes facing forward and two facing back, their feet can clamp into the bark, allowing the birds to shuffle up and down the tree headfirst. Both birds feed on insects wedged into the tree bark, so the added mobility allows them to

Once the osprey hoists its catch from the water with its meat-hook-like claws, it is able to turn the fish to position it face forward, thereby reducing the wind resistance for the long flight home.

attack their prey from any angle. The woodpecker, well known for spending its days drilling wood, is securely anchored while working.

The flexible feet of climbing and perching birds are not, however, a characteristic of ground-nesting birds such as the killdeer. Their feet are stout and strong—better suited for quick escapes—and their claws are extra long and sharp, especially useful for scratching a nest in the earth or digging up insects.

Flightless birds have shorter claws that will not interfere with their mobility, and while their heavily padded toes may be unsuitable for perching, their feet are tough and muscular and can withstand hours of roadwork. The roadrunner chases lizards, the mainstay of its diet, at speeds of up to 25 kilometres per hour, while the ostrich, the largest bird in the world, running at 50 kilometres per hour, is also the fastest—even its chick kicks up the dust at 30 kilometres per hour.

Waders need long, rather than strong, legs, which allow cranes, flamingos and herons to wade out into the water after their prey. Flamingos are filter feeders that dip their bills into the water and sift out their food, while cranes and herons stand motionless in shallow water, waiting to spear a fish. A wader's mobility is restricted, however, by its gangly legs, which are weak and are awkward in flight.

Highly specialized feet that work as paddles to propel them through the water make ducks, geese and loons strong swimmers. Their toes are webbed with a membrane of skin that provides a larger area for paddling and pushing against the water. Swamp birds such as the rail family, which includes gallinules and coots, have specially lobed, wide toes that keep the birds afloat as they race across lily pads and other floating swamp vegetation.

When you watch a bird, study its feet carefully. You will notice that a pigeon prances around on its stiff feet, which are too rigid for perching, while the robin has long, flexible toes that are perfect for hopping and perching. A bird's feet are a subtle reminder of how each bird species lives its own special life.

The aquatic horned puffin uses its three-toed webbed feet for steering and its wings for propulsion underwater.

A great blue heron's bill is like a long, sharp spear. When a heron goes fishing, it wades into the water and waits, watching for schools of fish to swim past. As its prey approaches, the heron slowly draws back its head; when a fish is within reach, the bird snaps its head forward and strikes with its bill, like an arrow shot from a bow.

A bill is much more than a food-gathering device, however. When birds evolved wings, they lost the ability to grasp and seize with their forelimbs. So the bill, combined with a highly mobile head, performs triple duty — it acts as mouth, teeth and paws all rolled into one. Composed of a durable material that is economical for the bird to produce, the bill is a bony core covered with keratin, the same protein found in feathers. The bill is used in grooming, courtship, defence, nestling care and nest construction. In spite of its hornlike composition, the bill can chip, crack and wear; like our fingernails, which are also made of keratin, it grows continuously.

You can tell a lot about a bird's diet by looking at its bill. There is a relationship between the design of a bill and what a bird eats. Raptors, or birds of prey, like the eagle, owl and hawk, have large, strong, hooked bills that bite and tear flesh while their feet immobilize the prey. The merganser, a fish-eating duck, has a serrated bill that is ideal for grasping a wriggling fish. The robin has a good all-purpose bill; strong and slightly elongated, it is suited to tugging big, fat, juicy worms out of the ground, eating fruit or grabbing insects. The short, broad bills of such insect-eaters as the swift, swallow and martin open wide to scoop up the weevils, wasps, moths and dragonflies they capture in flight. The blunt-tipped bills of the goose and swan are built for a life of grazing, allowing the birds to cut a great quantity of vegetation in a way that a sharp-billed species cannot. And that design is important because the low energy value of the grazer's diet means that it must be able to obtain a lot of food easily to sustain itself.

Some bills are suited to a particular type of food and foraging technique. The hummingbird has a long, specialized bill at least half the length of its body and a slender, tubular tongue that can reach deep inside a flower to lap up nectar. Hummingbirds can also pluck small flies out of the air by opening their bills and quickly snapping them closed like tweezers.

Birds such as the grouse, pheasant

With a lightning-fast jab of its head, a great blue heron can snatch a small fish from the water using its arrowlike bill.

and turkey have a muscular part of the stomach called a gizzard, which pulverizes, or crushes, hickory and acorn seeds. But some seed-eating birds must be able to break open the indigestible protective cover surrounding their food before they can eat the nutritious portion inside. The cardinal, the sparrow and the grosbeak – all members of the finch family – have heavy, cone-shaped bills that are strong enough to crush seedcases open, just as a nutcracker can. The crossbill, also a member of the finch family, is named for its stout, scissored bill. The bill holds the scales of a pine cone open, allowing the crossbill to reach in between the scales with its tongue and lift out the pine seeds.

With the exception of raptors, which have powerful feet and legs for carrying, all birds transport nest-building materials in their bills. The cliff swallow uses its bill as a trowel to mould and shape clay pellets into spherical nests. Songbirds carry twigs, grass, plant stems, moss and milkweed in their bills and then weave the materials into a cup-shaped structure. The flicker and woodpecker rely on their bills to chisel nest holes in tree trunks.

Like an elaborate dance or bright feathers, a bird's bill can also be important in courtship. During breeding season, some bills even change colour – the male robin's normally yellowish bill, for instance, intensifies to a dark gold. Other bills change shape and size. During courtship, the bills of the male and female puffin grow multicoloured plates, and the puffins use their bills

The blue jay has a stout, strong bill suited to prying seeds from a sunflower head and splitting open the shells.

to peck, nuzzle and rub one another. When breeding season is over, the birds shed the colourful plates just as they moult their feathers. Courting pairs of gannets and ravens perform billing, an affectionate display in which each pecks, nibbles, rubs and clasps the bill of its mate.

The bill is an essential part of a bird's gear – compact, lightweight, efficient and multipurpose. A good place to watch birds using their bills is around a feeder, where you will see blue jays, woodpeckers, sparrows, cardinals, nuthatches and chickadees in action, each with its own unique bill. Watch the grosbeaks that expertly crack and open sunflower seeds faster than any of the other birds; the blue jays that toss the seeds back into their crops; and the nuthatches that pick up sunflower seeds one by one and carry them back to a branch, where they wedge them into bark crevices to peck them open.

From its pine-tree perch, a bald eagle spots a flash of colour and movement a kilometre away. It fixes its stare on a distant clearing, and as it scans the ground, its large, contractible pupils adjust like a lens, quickly bringing into focus a white-tailed rabbit feeding on a patch of clover. Before the rabbit senses that it is a target, the eagle is airborne and swooping in for the kill.

Life on the wing places special demands on the senses. While most mammals experience the world primarily through scent and sound, birds rely heavily on vision not only to hunt and to escape danger but to feed, drink and build their nests. Flying animals travel quickly and must have reliable senses to prevent collisions.

Since most birds remain active during the day, many of their needs are best satisfied by good eyesight. All birds have large eyes that see colour; they can focus faster than humans can, and their eyesight is sharper. But because human eyes move inside their sockets, we have a wider field of vision. A bird's eyes are locked rigidly in their sockets, and its field of vision is therefore restricted. In other words, a bird cannot see from side to side without moving its head. To overcome that restriction, many species have unusually placed eyes.

The eyes of the American woodcock are positioned high up on the

Along with the other birds of prey — the owl, hawk, osprey and falcon — the bald eagle is a hunter and has forward-positioned eyes that give it powerful binocular vision.

sides of its head so that it has nearly a 360-degree field of vision. A ground-nesting species, the woodcock is able to see what is coming toward it as well as things approaching from behind, allowing it to escape the attacks of predators.

While the woodcock's attackers sneak up from behind, the American bittern must be on guard against predators that lurk beneath its feet in the swamps where it lives. To help protect it from attack, its eyes are set in the lower half of its head. Standing in the tall grasses of a marsh, the bittern freezes so that it is perfectly still yet is able to see beneath its body to avoid the muskrats and the minks which might attack it from below and to stalk the frogs, snakes, fish and insects it likes to eat. The risks of its restricted field of vision are offset by the overhead cover provided by the lofty marsh grasses, which conceal the bittern from aerial predators.

Many swimming and diving birds, such as ducks, have a nictitating membrane, or third eyelid, to improve their eyesight while they are hunting underwater. A thin membrane that lies beneath the exterior upper and lower eyelids and acts as an underwater face mask, the translucent third eyelid allows the bird to see even when the membrane is closed. In flight, many birds draw the membrane across their eyeballs to keep them moist and to protect them from dust and dirt.

The internal structure of the eye also varies among bird species. The retina contains cells that are receptors for vision, called rods and

A quick blink of the spectacled owl's translucent third eyelid, or nictitating membrane, keeps its eyeball clean and moist.

cones. The rods and cones, which contain pigments that are light-sensitive, convey impulses to the brain about both light and dark. Cones enable the bird to see shapes and colours in the bright light of day. Birds that hunt for small, motionless objects, like seeds, and for worms, which are partially hidden in the ground, have eyes that are rich in cones. Rods function at night or in low lighting; therefore, night-active birds, such as owls and whippoor-wills, have an abundance of them.

The vision of owls and whippoor-wills also profits from "nightshine" —a layer of cells behind the rod-and-cone section of the retina that gives the cornea a glossy, mirrorlike quality and captures much of the available light, allowing the bird to see detail where humans see only darkness. Listen and watch for these birds on nights when there is a full moon as they make the most of the bright moonlight.

A grooming mallard combs its feathers smooth and uses a waxy glandular secretion to keep them oiled and waterproof.

Carefully using its bill to draw beads of water over its coat, the mallard systematically cleans every feather from the back of its neck to the end of its tail. At first, all the filaments on the duck's plumage are ruffled and ragged-looking; after a meticulous combing, however, they are smooth, clean and oiled.

Nothing is more important to a bird than its feathers. Birds are the only animals that possess this unique design feature, and feathers are the key to a bird's success. Brilliantly engineered, lightweight and strong, firm yet flexible, feathers are not only warm and water-resistant but also vital to the creation of the large, smooth wing surface that enables birds to fly.

Feathers are made from filaments of protein woven together along a rigid, lightweight shaft. The shaft is a strong, hollow, tapered tube made from keratin, the same hornlike material which covers the bird's bill and from which your own hair and fingernails are made. As many as a million filaments lock tightly together along each shaft, providing insulation and protecting the bird from the rain and the sun.

Birds have a variety of feathers, which develop at a different rate in each species. There are down, flight, ornamental, semiplume and contour feathers. When many birds hatch, they are covered with a complete layer of fluffy down that helps them blend in with their surroundings. But, unlike sleek adult plumage, down feathers are fuzzy and stand on end to trap warm air and provide extra insulation for the vulnerable young bird. Most songbirds hatch naked and remain in the nest under the care of their parents until they grow their first, or juvenile, feathers. A young bird's first true feathers often provide camouflage and give it additional protection. Bald eagles wear juvenile plumage until they are almost 4 years old and fully able to defend themselves, a mate and a territory.

Feather pigments come in a variety of colours. Skin pigment, which can be influenced by both heredity and hormones, affects the colour of the feathers. The yellow and red carotenoid plants that a bird eats are converted into the red pigments which colour the plumage. Shrimp contains the same pigment that makes carrots orange; when shrimp is a regular item in the flamingo's diet, the colour builds up in the feathers and gives them an incredibly pink hue. When shrimp is not available, the flamingo's feathers often lose their colour.

Other colours are structural, pro-

To bathe its body in the soft sand, a house sparrow churns the dirt to create a dust cloud that sifts through its feathers.

duced by layers in the feather material that reflect some colours and trap others. Peacock and humming bird feathers have surface hairs, called barbules, that interfere with the projection of light across the plumage, creating an iridescent display of colours.

Feathers play an important role in a bird's social life. Nighthawks and hummingbirds rustle their feathers in a territorial or threat display, while peacocks and boat-tailed grackles parade their huge, fanned, ornamental feathers during courtship. But birds pay a high price for elaborate ornamental feathers, which can attract unwanted attention and restrict mobility. Peacocks are easy targets for predators. While male songbirds usually wear decorative plumage, the females tend

to be dull-coloured and thus can conceal themselves while they are incubating their eggs.

Given all these functions, it is no wonder that birds take special care of their feathers with regular preening and cleaning. Birds rub their feathers with oil produced by a gland at the base of the tail, thereby improving their moisture resistance but retaining their insulating value.

Water birds have the most well-developed oil glands, but many ducks, when deprived of these glands, can still maintain a water-repellent coat. This has led scientists to believe that the water resistance may actually be built right into the feather itself. Other species that have reduced glands keep their plumage water-resistant with

The rock ptarmigan moults for winter camouflage.

The backlighting from a sunset outlines the softly curved courtship plumage on the back of a snowy egret. Human greed for the flawless plumage nearly wiped out the egret population in this century.

an oil-rich diet of seeds and nuts.

Even with all this attention, feathers do not last forever. Just like any well-worn clothing, they take a beating. The daily wear and tear caused by flying among and into tree branches exacts its toll, and eventually, feathers must be replaced. By the end of the demanding breeding season, fatigue is outwardly visible in a bird's tattered plumage. Each year after the breeding season, but while the weather is still warm, a bird sheds and replaces its feathers.

There are thousands of specialized bird pests whose sole purpose is to abuse bird feathers. Bloodsucking insects crawl beneath the plumage and puncture the skin, while mites nibble at the feathers. Although a well-oiled coat may help to fight off the pests that live on bird feathers, many shorebirds and seabirds take periodic dives into the water to wash them away, while sparrows have gritty dust baths to remove parasites. Nicotine is a powerful insecticide, and blue jays have been known to wipe their feathers with cold cigarette butts. The defensive chemicals secreted by ants are thought to repel feather mites, fleas and lice, and some birds have been observed rubbing ants on their feathers in an apparent attempt to remove the annoying pests.

While grooming helps to reduce feather and skin parasites, birds also have a few built-in pest-control systems. The purpose of some feathers is simply to grow and crumble so that they can be spread throughout the plumage like a fine dusting pow-

A bead of water provides a magnified glimpse of the hooked barbules that lock the gull's feather vanes together.

der, cleaning the feathers. To help pick mites and bugs out of their coats and to keep their feathers looking neat and the filaments flat, some birds have a feather comb, a special toothed claw positioned on one toe. Since the top of the head and the back of the neck are the only two places on the body that a bird cannot reach on its own, pairs of birds often preen one another.

When you see a bird, whether you are in a park or at home, pay at-tention to how much time it spends caring for its feathers. If you find a feather that a bird has lost during its moult, pick it up and run your finger over the filaments to separate them. When you smooth the feather vanes in the direction of the tip, you will find that you can relock the vanes, as though you were closing a zipper. When a bird grooms, it smooths the filaments of its own feathers, taking care of one of its most vital possessions.

A hummingbird can zoom up to a flower at 40 kilometres per hour and stop in an instant, hovering motionless as it inserts its bill into the blossom and laps up the nectar. At more than 50 times a second, its wings beat so fast that they appear to be just a buzzing blur.

A hummingbird's light weight allows it to specialize in hovering flight and agile aerial manoeuvres – it can dive straight down, soar upwards or sheer sideways; it can even fly backwards. The hummingbird moves in ways that heavier birds can never match. Yet even for the tiny, lightweight bird – it might take 200 individuals to weigh one kilogram – hovering is physically demanding. Its heart pumps 1,260 times per minute and is, relative to body weight, the largest heart of all birds. Its chest muscles make up 30 percent of its mass, and hovering taxes this machinery to its limit.

Each species of bird has its own specialized form of flight. The energy output required for hovering far exceeds what large birds such as herons, eagles, hawks, vultures and storks could produce. In order to fly efficiently, a large-bodied bird conserves its energy and maximizes its opportunity for flight by using its enormous wings to glide and soar like a paper kite. The wings of inland soaring birds such as raptors are rectangular-shaped, both long and wide, to catch thermals – pockets of air that rise from the Earth's surface when the ground is warmed by the midday sun. Ocean-soaring birds, like albatrosses, have long, narrow, oar-shaped wings that, although large, are compact and better suited to the gusting, turbulent winds which blow over open water.

Flight is without a doubt the most exciting form of locomotion, and humans have struggled for centuries to copy what birds can do naturally. But it is also an energy-consuming way to get around. Birds must wage a constant battle with gravity and friction, the same two forces that humans must overcome in order to launch an airplane.

Takeoff is a demanding prelude to flight because it requires a downward thrust of air that must be strong enough to overcome the force of gravity, and the weight of many birds means that they cannot become airborne from a standing start. Some birds catch a gust of wind to lift them into the air by taking a running start or by leaping from a perch. The loon, a powerful flier, is unable to launch itself from dry land and must therefore taxi hundreds of metres along a watery runway, arching its back and gradually pulling up its chest before it has enough speed to lift off.

The force of lift that boosts a bird into the air is created by the airflow over and around its wings. Lift is created when air moves faster over the top of the wing than it does under the wing, and it is the curved profile of a bird's wing that causes the air to flow at different speeds across the surfaces. The upper surface is convex, so air flows faster over the top than it does on the underside. The result is a difference in air pressure, and the slower airstream, which passes under the

In one second, the stripe-tailed hummingbird can beat its wings more than 50 times, enabling it to hover while feeding.

wing, buoys, or lifts, the wing as it moves through the atmosphere.

When a bird slows down for a landing, it is necessary for it to maintain a sufficient airflow over its wings or, just as an aircraft might, it will stall. The design of a bird's wings helps it adapt to changing speed in two ways. First, it can alter the speed of the airflow over the wing by using the primary feathers near the tip of the wing, called the alula. Like an airplane's flaps, the alula can be raised, lowered or twisted to increase or decrease the speed at which air passes over the top of the wings. Second, a bird can change the shape of its wings and increase their surface to provide a greater area of lift. Feathers can be spread or folded like fingers, thereby allowing a bird to add to or reduce the surface area available for lift and so adjust to changing winds.

Friction also affects flight, but the shape of a wing helps to reduce it. A wing's forward edge is blunt and the tail side is tapered by the feathers so that the wind passes smoothly over the top. But some small birds, like swallows and swifts, further reduce the wind resistance caused by their bodies and wings by using bounding flight. They pump their wings in frenetic spurts and then streamline their bodies and stretch their necks out straight to make them long and narrow. By folding their wings tightly against their bodies, they can shoot through the air like arrows, with little resistance.

But birds that neither bound nor soar must use flapping flight, which, after hovering, is the most strenu-

The pintail duck's large wing area compared with its body size helps it to spring directly into flight from the surface of a pond.

ous form of flight. To reduce the energy cost of flapping flight, Canada geese fly in a V formation, which allows each bird to take advantage of the reduced wind resistance behind the lead birds. Also, to avoid turbulence, they fly at high altitudes. Both techniques save energy.

One of the most reliable ways to identify a bird is to learn its characteristic flight pattern. The slowly flapping wings of the heron, the whirling helicopter flight of the hummingbird, the fixed-wing soaring of raptors and the swooping, bounding flight of swallows and swifts will help you to recognize what sort of bird you see flying high in the sky.

Courtship

The sage grouse woos mates at a lek, a mating theatre where the male huffs and puffs his way through courtship. Inflating a feathered chest sac and strutting around, whistling, stomping and fighting with other males, a dominant male proves his worth when he manages to take control of the centre stage, a patch of ground in the area. Year after year, hundreds of males will return to these sites to perform their courtship displays.

Females from surrounding territories gather at a lek and carefully assess each performance. The male that makes the greatest impression of strength is rewarded by being allowed to father almost all the offspring. Since the female sage grouse must be responsible for egg production, nest building, egg laying and parental care, it is in her best interests to mate with a superior male, one that is strong and without disease or defect.

With very few exceptions, a male bird has more chances to sire offspring than a female has to produce them, but first, the male must convince a female to choose him. Therefore, he initiates courtship, focusing his energy on elaborate displays that prove his worth.

The decorative plumage of a male bird is another courtship display. Brightly coloured, glamorous plumage, which has evolved as the criterion for mate selection, signals that the male is healthy, strong and perhaps able to provide good genes for the offspring. A male bird usually develops colourful plumage only when he is sexually mature and able to defend a territory and a family. Adult peacocks and many duck species wear their colours year-round, while other species may have them only during the mating season.

Other courting behaviours reveal the male's willingness to offer practical help or resources to the nesting female. The short-billed marsh wren and the red-winged blackbird use a good-quality territory to attract females. Both species inhabit densely overgrown marshy areas with rich food supplies and nest sites that offer protection from predators, something not available in all habitats. The male marsh wren builds many nests throughout his territory and offers each female her choice. The more nests the male constructs, the better his chances of finding a mate; if he is an accomplished builder, he may attract more than one female.

Rather than trying to secure

Hens at the sage grouse lek select the superior male, on the basis of his courtship display, to father all of their offspring.

several partners during courtship, many seabirds, crows, pigeons and members of the heron family use mutual preening to interact with just one partner. Preening and billing, which consist of delicate combing and rubbing around the head and neck, serve the practical purpose of grooming. A pair of birds uses the technique during courtship to develop familiarity and to confirm their partnership. For birds that have to work in a coordinated manner to rear their offspring, it is an important ritual.

Some birds use their bills in courtship displays. The male green heron raises his head and bill vertically in an action that shows his intentions to females, while the bills of the puffin grow larger and more colourful during breeding season.

During courtship, birds are often so preoccupied with attracting a mate that they are oblivious to all other concerns. At such times, they are more easily approached. Observing birds as they choose their partners makes for some of the most entertaining bird watching.

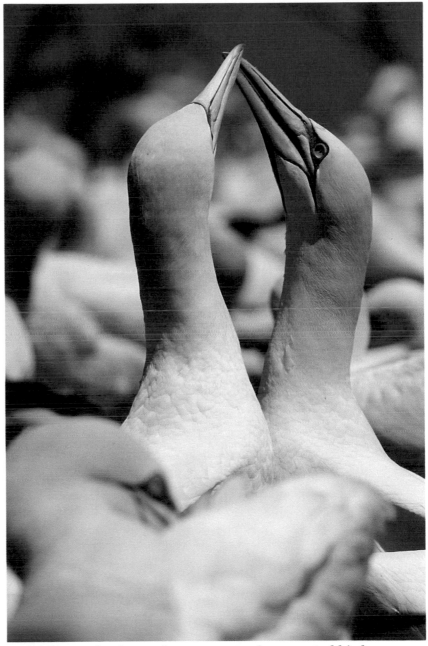

Amid the crush of a northern gannet colony, mated birds maintain their bond by repeatedly rapping their bills.

After months at sea, a pair of wandering albatrosses comes ashore to reaffirm its lifelong bond. Standing beside the nest mound, the male points his head and bill skyward and greets his mate with open wings. Their courtship may go on for days before they mate successfully, and since fledging their young can take up to 12 months – clearly a long-term commitment – albatrosses breed only in alternate years.

While few birds maintain the kind of long-lasting relationship that the albatross family does, 95 percent of all birds mate with only one partner during the breeding season, a system biologists refer to as "monogamous," meaning one partner. The monogamous pairing occurs most often when both parents are needed to defend and care for the eggs and young hatchlings as well as to feed the hungry chicks. In families of raptors and seabirds, when one partner must leave the nest to forage for food, the other remains behind to protect the nest from predators and aggressive neighbours. For songbirds, which produce large clutches of offspring, monogamy is a necessity. While the hatchlings are developing, one parent alone would not be able to keep them warm, guard the nest and hunt for the insects and worms required to feed five or six nestlings.

The female clearly benefits from the assistance of a full-time mate,

Monogamous wandering albatrosses come ashore every other year to breed. Only death or a bird divorce, caused by repeated nest or breeding failure, can break the lifelong bond of the albatross.

but the advantages for the male are less obvious. When a male establishes a bond with a single female, he invests all his time in a few offspring and reduces his opportunities for reproduction. But for the male seabird or raptor, monogamy is a way to guard his mate from the sexual advances of rival males. Rather than effectively restricting reproductive opportunities, monogamy is a way of ensuring that the offspring the male cares for are truly his own.

If a male can control a territory that contains lots of food and has good nesting sites, he is able to support more than one partner. Such relationships are called "polygynous," meaning many females, and they occur most often in rich, easily defended habitats, such as marshes and swamps. In exchange for a nest site and an abundant food supply in a well-guarded habitat, females like the red-winged blackbird and the short-billed marsh wren often share a male with other females. The arrangement does not eliminate competition for a place within a male's territory, however. Established females have been observed doing their best to prevent new females from joining the harem.

The number of offspring that each bird can yield is often limited by the egg-producing capabilities of the female and by the abilities of the parents to feed their offspring. But in habitats that provide a reliable and nutritious food supply year-round, a female has both the energy to lay more than one clutch of eggs and the food to nourish the nestlings. Some

Prior to the mating season, wild turkeys engage in fierce competition to determine which male will court all the hens.

sandpipers and water birds, like the tropical jaçana, form "polyandrous" pairs, partnerships in which the female mates with many males, each of which is responsible for the care of his own offspring.

When male parental care for the female's many egg clutches is so much in demand, fierce fighting occurs between females for available mates. Polyandrous females are thus larger than males and more aggressive and territorial while breeding. We generally assume males are the brightly coloured, outgoing sex, but keep in mind that a bird's mating behaviour is influenced by its environment.

With only its eyes visible through a knothole, a screech owl is secure in its wooden fortress. Its nest is a modest lodging, neither smoothly excavated nor amply lined with bedding materials. But the rough-grained tree trunk keeps the owl safe from predators and sheltered from the wind, rain and cold.

Nests are, first and foremost, a place to lay and incubate eggs and to raise nestlings. Since positioning the nest in a safe location is the best way for most birds to protect their young, it is no wonder that many birds, such as chickadees and owls, will fight to control natural tree cavities and abandoned woodpecker holes. But most birds use flight to position their nests high in a tree, where the location provides built-in security. The Baltimore oriole takes

extra precautions: its nest is elevated and positioned on the outermost tip of a tree branch, where only the most agile predator can creep. The hummingbird camouflages its nest with bits of moss and chips of bark, making it difficult to spot among the tree's leaves.

Birds most vulnerable to attack sometimes build the least elaborate structures. Ground-nesting birds, like the sage grouse, have little natural protection from nest-robbing snakes, foxes, raccoons, badgers and birds, yet they lay their eggs in a simple scrape in the ground. While the nests are not secure or particularly warm, the casual design seems to work, perhaps because a woven nest on the ground would only draw attention to the eggs. During incubation, the textured plumage of the

ground-nesting parent helps to protect it, and when the bird leaves the nest to feed, the coloured eggs blend perfectly with the surroundings.

Most birds construct warm, insulated structures that will contain their body heat during incubation. Many nests are delicately woven and are shaped so that they are just large enough to hold the brooding bird and the eggs; any extra room would allow warmth to escape. The hummingbird's cup-style nest is a masterpiece of thermal engineering. While smaller than a teacup, the nest is deep and has thick walls that are heavily padded with cattail down to contain all the precious heat generated by the hummingbird to warm its eggs.

Birds living under the heat of the desert sun, however, spend less time incubating their eggs and more time keeping them cool and shaded. To counteract the effects of temperatures that regularly climb above 40 degrees C, the white-winged dove designs a ventilated nest of sticks and twigs loosely piled together to release, rather than contain, the heat. The eggs of the Gila woodpecker survive the Arizona sun in a cool nest hollowed out of the moist core of a desert cactus, where the sun cannot penetrate. In a process called belly-soaking, desert-dwelling members of the plover family bathe their abdominal feathers in water and return to the nest to rub the water over their eggs to keep them from overheating.

There are many kinds of bird nests—cup, platform, cavity, pendulous and adherent—and each is

Windproof and waterproof, sturdy and easy to defend, a natural cavity provides the nest of choice for the screech owl.

After collecting a billful of sea grasses for nesting material, the male northern gannet returns to the colony and ceremoniously drops it on the female's head, a ritual that strengthens their pair bond.

constructed from natural materials such as grass, straw, mud, spider silk and even bird saliva. The challenge each bird faces is to work with materials found in its habitat and to come up with a design that is suitable for the environment in which it lives. The cliff swallow lives high on the rocky face of a cliff, and it builds a fully enclosed, windproof, water-resistant mud shelter that adheres to the vertical surface. The robin weaves its grassy cup on a solid base of mud that secures it to a branch, just as a concrete foundation supports a house. Likewise, the hummingbird, which builds the tiniest of all nests and therefore the one most vulnerable to the wind, binds it together with spider silk, the strongest material in nature. The yellow warbler, however, weaves its cup-style nest out of material that can be found in a number of habitats.

When the leaves have fallen from the trees, bird nests are easy to find. Nests in trees and shrubs are usually not reused, so you can gently remove one, pull it apart and study the remarkable collection of materials that birds use to create a design which works for them.

Cradling a set of fresh eggs, a robin's nest tucked in the branch of a tree is one of the most beautiful sights on Earth. Not only is robin's-egg blue a colour of unmatched elegance, but each egg is itself a marvel of biological engineering. Enclosed within a single protective case are cells carrying the mysterious genetic instructions that will build a living animal.

From the bean-sized hummingbird egg to the boulder-sized egg of the now extinct elephant bird, eggs come in as many colours, shapes and sizes as do the birds that lay them. Easy to spot in the wild, white eggs are laid only by birds that have safe or concealed nests: the woodpecker constructs a nest in the security of a hollowed-out tree trunk, where its white eggs are hidden from view; the hummingbird can conceal its pair of tiny eggs with its body; and the ground-nesting mallard carefully covers its white eggs with vegetation when leaving its nest unattended.

But for birds which build open cup-style nests or which lay their eggs in a shallow scrape on the ground, white eggs would be an easy meal for any passing predator. Such birds lay a variety of well-disguised, speckled, coloured eggs that blend in with the surroundings. The egg's colour is determined as it passes through the oviduct and either haemoglobin, which provides the brown tones, or bile, which creates the green tones, is released into the shell. Ground-nesting birds such as the grouse and the woodcock lay spotted, camouflaged eggs

The turquoise colour of the robin's egg comes from haemoglobin and bile that are deposited in the shell as it is being formed.

that are completely invisible among the leaves and grass on the forest floor, while the turquoise hue of a robin's egg in the shade makes it almost indistinguishable from the leaves of the tree in which the nest is built.

As egg colour has evolved to suit the egg's surroundings, so has its shape. Most eggs are oval, which provides added strength and allows the maximum surface area of the shell to be covered by the bird's body during incubation. But gulls, auks and murres lay cone-shaped eggs that are very tapered at one end so that they will not roll but will turn in a circle when moved. These birds are cliff nesters, and such an adaptation prevents the eggs from rolling off the cliff.

Like mollusk shells, chalk and our

own bones, an eggshell is composed of calcium carbonate. The waterproof covering contains tiny pores that allow oxygen to pass to the inside so that the embryo can breathe. The fertilized embryo is bathed in egg white, or albumen, which is sealed with a rubbery membrane that lines the shell. This essential moisture, which amphibian and fish eggs obtain from being deposited in water, is contained inside each individually wrapped package, called an amniotic egg.

The living bird begins as an embryo, a tiny reddish blob of protoplasm on the top of the large yolk. While the embryo remains in the shell, the yolk sac, which is a golden mixture of proteins, fats and carbohydrates, provides the nourishment that it needs to grow. The yolk and the white of the egg are kept separate by the fine vitelline membrane, the same membrane that holds the yolk together in a fried egg. As the egg warms during incubation, the embryo grows, its cells begin to multiply and the ratio of embryo to yolk and albumen changes. By the end of its time in the shell, the embryo has used up all its food and all the liquid in the shell. Once this happens, it is time to hatch.

While production of the amniotic egg is physically demanding, the success rate for most birds is high compared with that of other egg-laying animals, and as a result, birds lay fewer eggs. While fish and insects must produce thousands, and in some cases millions, of eggs to offset their failure rate, few birds lay more than 15 eggs per clutch.

The availability of food can affect the number of eggs that a bird lays. A parent must spend a great deal of time hunting to find enough food to fill the hungry mouth of a carnivorous eagle or hawk nestling, which may explain why raptors rear few or no offspring in some years and why seabirds rarely lay more than two eggs.

A penguin's egg production is limited by the demands of incubating an egg in the Antarctic cold. An emperor penguin must incubate its egg for more than two months, cradling the egg on the top of its feet and carrying it everywhere it goes to shield it from the cold, something the brooding parent clearly could not do with many eggs.

The penguin's hard work highlights the one drawback of the amniotic egg—it requires constant care. While amphibian and fish eggs can be left to hatch heated by the warmth of the sun, a bird's egg needs direct incubation from the hot, blood-filled crest, or brood patch, that appears on the chest of the attending parent. To help conserve the heat produced during incubation, many birds take on the task of building a nest, where the egg is cared for by the adult until the chick hatches.

Few things are as simple, familiar and yet fascinating as an egg. The chicken egg, which millions of people routinely scramble, fry or boil every morning, is one of the neglected marvels of the natural world. At once, it represents the beginning and the future of all avian life.

To allow for maximum coverage during the incubation period, the eggs of the Baird's sandpiper are pear-shaped.

American goldfinch chicks struggling to break out of their shells look as if they are attempting to enter the world too early. Covered with sparse tufts of fuzz, the hatchlings are pink, blind and nearly naked; their eyes are just two black bumps fully grown over with skin. As they grope around the nest, it is difficult for an onlooker to imagine that they will be strong enough to fly on their own in just a few weeks.

Without parental care, the offspring of songbirds, raptors and many other species could not survive. Known as altricial birds, they are born in a completely helpless state, dependent on adults for warmth, food and protection until they are able to leave the nest. But the length of time offspring require such dedication from their parents varies from species to species. The robin spends a few weeks feeding its offspring; the young bald eagle may remain with its parents for nearly two months, while the immature wandering albatross stays in the nest for nine months.

The amount of time that a young bird remains under its parents' care is often determined by the availability of food and the ease with which the parents can obtain it. Raptors, for example, are hunters and must spend hours tracking their prey. The hard work of providing fish and small mammals for hungry nestlings keeps the parents out in the open all day and at risk. Each parent shares the demands of full-time parenthood, however, taking turns hunting and guarding the nest during the long hours spent foraging.

The female American goldfinch constructs a bowl-shaped nest packed with plant down to house her helpless chicks.

If it requires the efforts of both parents to fledge many altricial nestlings, it is, at first glance, curious that with the tiny ruby-throated hummingbird, the female is entirely responsible for the care of her altricial young. But she lays only two eggs. She uses high-energy food —nectar and insects—to feed her offspring. Since food is relatively abundant in summer, the female hummingbird alone is less likely to draw predators to the nest.

The noisy chirping of baby birds is attention-grabbing, and the longer a family stays in one location, the more likely the chance that it will be discovered by predators. Geese, woodcocks, ducks and all ground-nesting birds have little protection from attack by a fox or a snake, so once their precocial young, which hatch in an advanced state, emerge from the shell, the hatchlings head straight for the nearest open water or to a covered area to hide. Precocial birds take twice as long to incubate as do most songbirds, and when the eggs hatch, the nestlings are already covered with a protective down and are able to feed themselves by pecking seeds from the ground. During the time these birds spend with their parents, they learn to swim and forage on their own. But the adults still protect their offspring when necessary – if threatened, chicks of the loon and the grebe are quickly scooped up under the wing of a watchful parent and whisked away to safety.

Some birds provide no direct parental care. The mallee fowl, which belongs to a family that includes the Australian brush turkey, lays its eggs in a mound of rotting vegetation, where the heat from the decomposing vegetable matter incubates them. These birds are on their own once they hatch; they scramble up to the surface of the mound and make their way to the nearest thicket of scrub grass.

Rather than lavishing great care on their eggs, a few species lay eggs in another bird's nest. Known as brood parasitism, such behaviour is frequently practised by the cowbird. By freeing herself of the responsibility of building a nest and feeding and caring for her hatchlings, the cowbird is able to lay as many as 40 eggs per breeding season – a great number when you consider that the average bird lays only 100 eggs during its entire life.

From courtship through nest building to the day the eggs hatch, reproduction is a long, demanding process that is rewarded only if a

For three weeks, the female rufous hummingbird pumps her hatchlings full of regurgitated insects and nectar.

number of healthy offspring leave the nest. It requires a great deal of effort to launch offspring into the world, and each parent bird must either pay early, with time-consuming, slow-growing eggs, or pay later, with lots of parental care.

If you can find a nest and not disturb the parents, it is worth sitting quietly and watching the traffic. Many common birds, like robins, phoebes, starlings and barn swallows, can all be readily observed. The continuous effort of the parents to find food and the constant demands of the nestlings will give you a real appreciation of the amount of work that goes into producing each new generation.

Standing upright on a fallen tree, a male ruffed grouse digs his claws firmly into the bark for balance and begins to drum his wings slowly, producing a thumping sound. From the blur of the beating feathers comes a courtship signal, low and booming, like the rumbling of distant thunder, that will attract female ruffed grouse from a distance of several kilometres. Like the male woodpecker, which declares courtship intentions, territorial occu-pancy and aggression by drumming its bill on resonant trees, the male ruffed grouse communicates without using his voice.

Communication can be many things: an exaggerated, emotional, colourful display exchanged between individuals whose purpose is to alter one another's behaviour; a signal, a smell or a sound used to attract or appease a mate or to repel or intimidate a rival. While humans cannot readily perceive the scents and vibrations with which many other animals communicate, we are able to hear most of the sounds birds make and can listen to the rich, and often complex, messages they express.

Most birds sing using sound produced in the syrinx, a chamber in the windpipe. Songbirds, the most musical birds in the world, have the largest and the greatest variety of syringeal muscles. Using their throat muscles to control the tension within the chamber and the pressure of air within the lungs, birds adjust the volume, pitch and intensity of the sound to produce a wide array of signals that can have many meanings. Bird calls do more than just attract mates or repel rivals; they can also be used to maintain contact in dense vegetation and to issue warning or mobbing calls.

Courtship and territorial songs are complex compositions of notes that are typically performed by the male during mating season. In some species, like the marsh wren or mockingbird, the more songs the male knows and the better he sings them, the more impressive he appears in courtship and the more intimidating he is in territorial defence.

Many birds sing several different songs. Male long- and short-billed marsh wrens, for example, increase their repertoire every year and, by so doing, appear to have the largest harems and to be least likely to have their territories invaded by rivals. A large repertoire of songs may be the male's way of providing important information about himself, such as age and experience.

The male ruffed grouse furiously beats his wings to repel rivals and to attract the females within his territory.

Throughout the breeding season, the flicker drums its chisellike bill on the trunk of its favourite resonant tree to claim its territory and to attract or call to its mate.

A crowing barnyard rooster rules the roost, keeping his harem of hens close to home and warning them when danger is near.

That may explain why many species imitate the songs of other birds. Starlings and mockingbirds increase the size of their repertoires by copying the songs of their older, more experienced neighbours, as do young male indigo buntings. When imitation makes a male appear more experienced than he actually is, he is able to keep intruders out of his territory and therefore stands a better chance of attracting and then protecting a mate.

But many bird vocalizations are not related to mating and are neither complex nor musical. Small birds and ground-dwelling birds that are constantly threatened by predators have devised a system of alarm calls with which to warn others in the territory. The bird sounding the alarm lets out short, sharp cries to expose the predator, but because the calls are difficult to pinpoint, there are few clues to help the predator locate the signaller.

Other warning calls are designed to attract the attention of the attacker. When a jay spots a predator, it lets out a long, loud cry. The call tells the intruder that it has been seen and that there is no chance for a surprise attack. A rooster dramatically draws attention to himself as he warns his brood of a raptor overhead. But not all alarm calls are given so unselfishly. Some birds use their cries to flush other inhabitants of the territory out of hiding and into the jaws of an attacker, while they wait for an opportunity to escape.

Songbirds such as chickadees and warblers confront nest-robbing birds like crows with chattering, buzzing and mobbing calls. The calls attract other songbirds, and together, they attack, peck and harass the intruder. It is common for house sparrows to gather on a power line to scold a cat creeping through the hedges.

Since vocalization is largely about territory and courtship, female songbirds sing less than males. But females do vocalize. When a female robin sits on the nest and warbles faintly in a duet with her mate, she affirms the pair bond, which helps them to defend their territory as well as to coordinate the feeding of the nestlings. While singing near the nest site has its risks, the ever watchful male ensures that the female is not courted by another.

As the sun breaks through the morning sky, choruses of birds court and claim territory at the top of their voices. Bird watchers spend a lot of time learning bird songs, because it is often easier to recognize a particular bird's song than to spot and identify the bird. In the spring and summer breeding seasons, birds rise early to perform their songs; it is the best time of day to appreciate the incredible range and variety of bird songs and sounds.

While the barn swallow's spring pronouncement can be a cheerful, fluttering melody, this barn swallow appears to recoil in pain in reaction to the loud, shrill cry of its mate.

A peacock displays his genetic qualities by parading his spectacular matrimonial plumage before a potential mate.

With the rainbow-coloured side of his train flopped forward over his head, a peacock waits for a hen to approach. When she nears, he suddenly spins around to display his shimmering blue chest and the iridescent eyespots that stare out from each of his fanned tail feathers. The female is momentarily hypnotized by the performance, and the peacock lunges forward to surround her with his courtship plumage. But she dashes beyond his reach, forcing him to perform the ritual again before they can mate.

This courtship dance of the peacock is an example of a specialized kind of bird communication known as a display ritual. Following a fixed sequence of postures, movements and calls, the displays are a precise, effective form of communication. Virtually all threat, courtship and territorial expressions used by birds are ritualized performances.

Ritual displays are based on natural behaviours that, through repetition, have become obvious signals of intention. Why a display becomes ritualized can be partly explained by reading the information that each action contains. When a rival approaches, a bald eagle displays aggression by ruffling its feathers, spreading its wings and pushing its powerful bill forward in a threatening pose to exaggerate its size; but that display is also an accurate imitation of an eagle about to fight. It is a straightforward, clear warning of hostility and threat and, as such, may benefit the eagle by discouraging a rival before combat becomes necessary. Whenever a bird can make a convincing display by simply flexing its muscles, it avoids the danger of having to prove its strength in a fight and saves time and energy.

As part of the courtship ritual of the cedar waxwing, the male pops berries into the female's mouth. While the male's intention is to be chosen as a mate, such a display may have evolved as a demonstration of the male's ability to feed nestlings, a trait that would make him a useful partner.

The meaning of the message is determined to some degree by its audience. When a male red-winged blackbird flashes its bright red epaulets, a rival male sees a threat and may either avoid the territory or risk a fight. But the display carries a different message to a female red-wing. She sees a strong, experienced and territorial male that might make a good mate because he is able to keep predators and rivals away, and so she might respond to the dis-

Passing a ripe berry back and forth is a ritualized courtship display among cedar waxwings that strengthens their bond.

play as if it were a courtship signal.

With his neck extended forward, parallel to the ground, the male Canada goose swings his head from side to side calling *A-honk*, *A-honk*, *A-hink*. The female, head tilted at an angle, alternates the male's call with a high-pitched *hink, hink, hink*. Humans use ceremonial greetings such as shaking hands, waving or smiling at one another when they meet. Birds use greeting ceremonies as well. This display is performed by mated pairs of Canada geese every time they see each other.

While most displays have evolved as a way for birds to interact with other birds, the killdeer's broken-wing performance is a defensive attempt to distract predators. Long before you find a killdeer nest in an open field, you might hear a killdeer

whimpering pathetically. Dragging a leg or a wing as though it were injured, the killdeer will hobble a safe distance away from the nest. But don't expect to catch the bird. Every time it suspects that a fox or a weasel might be nearby hunting for a nest, the killdeer performs this exaggerated ritual to draw the predator away. The display is all the more believable because the killdeer has a reddish spot resembling a blood-stain near the base of its tail.

Killdeer are common in open, gravelly areas. If you can visit such a habitat in spring and find a killdeer, it is an excellent way to experience the convincing, dramatic and emotional power of ritual behaviour.

The killdeer's broken-wing display distracts predators.

Securely plastered onto a branch with a mud foundation, the neatly shaped robin's nest, with its thick, high walls of sun-bleached grasses and pine needles, is a familiar sight. But it becomes something quite remarkable when you consider that year after year, every young North American robin, from the tree line of the Canadian northwest to the south of Mexico, builds exactly the same kind of structure without any help from its parents.

Birds are born knowing how to do certain things, and the ability to construct a nest is one such essential behaviour, or instinct. When a bird hatches, it is already too late for it to learn everything it needs to know in order to survive, and instincts, which are passed on by genes from one generation to the next, give the bird a head start. Already wired into the brain, instinctive reactions are fast and efficient, since they do not require the neural circuitry necessary for information storage.

Where predators are concerned, it pays to rely on instincts. Learning about natural enemies through experience may be dangerous. In response, animals evolve a variety of life-saving instincts. For instance, nestling chicks hide their heads when they see a black shape flying above because they are instinctively afraid of bird-eating hawks.

But while some instincts provide quick responses, instincts that are closed to the input of new information can lead a bird astray. During the breeding season, an adult male robin sees a rival in every red object, which it interprets as the red breast of another male. It will attack a puppet, a ball of feathers or even its own reflection, because it reacts instinctively not to the shape or the size of a rival but to its colour. Rather than helping to protect its mate and offspring, however, such a rigid response puts the robin at an unnecessary risk of injury every time it attacks an imaginary rival. Luckily, at breeding time, there are very few red objects in nature other than male robins. Apples and berries do not ripen until much later.

Humans have devised ways to take advantage of birds' instinctive fears. Gardeners keep songbirds from eating vegetables and flowers by laying rubber snakes throughout the gardens. A dummy owl placed on the roof or in a window prevents pigeons and swallows from building nests under eave troughs. And a scarecrow in a cornfield frightens away pesky magpies and crows.

Completely rigid behaviours are

The female robin's architectural instinct keeps her gathering the mud and pliable grasses necessary to build her nest.

few, however, and a bird's good-sized brain accepts new information that can influence its behaviour. Many birds increase their nest-building skills over time, improvising with materials and even adapting their architectural style to new environments. When a bird improves its foraging technique and learns to hunt more effectively, it also increases its food supply and its ability to feed a mate and offspring. Any bird that can manage in un-usual conditions or outside its natural habitat has a greater chance of survival.

Most behaviours are a combination of instinct and learning. You can see proof of that by hanging a hummingbird feeder in your backyard in the summer. Many feeders are designed with red plastic flowers at the spouts, a colourful display to which the tiny bird is instinctively attracted. But even with the benefit of such a cue, a hum-mingbird will hover around the feeder, banging its bill against the plastic as it tries again and again to get at the sugary water. You will see that after a little investigation, though, the bird eventually learns how to extract the nectar.

With practice, this 6½-week-old cygnet will eventually learn to imitate the renowned territorial, mating and triumph displays performed by its trumpeter swan parent.

Territories

Anchored to the tallest plant stem in the marsh, a male red-winged blackbird flashes a warning to an approaching bird that this is occupied territory. It is a convincing display – the jet-black bill, eyes, feet and body feathers contrast dramatically with the brilliant red epaulets that stand out boldly when the bird spreads his wings.

Defending a territory is a major occupation for most male birds. A territory is a space that can be used for nesting or a food source or both, and males compete to acquire one. Birds are often forced to protect their territories from predators that might attack their offspring, and they use threat displays and calls and even give chase to drive intruders away. But more often, birds must defend their territories against rivals from their own species.

Male migratory birds are often the first to arrive at the summer breeding grounds to select a territory. A carefully guarded territory provides a bird with a known range and with the resources that it contains. In many species, the male's ability to establish a safe territory with a rich food supply can be used to lure a mate. A breeding territory must be large enough to serve the needs of the male and his family but not so large that it is impossible to defend.

A territory's size varies for each bird. Some birds have a fixed territory, while others expand and re-

In a threat display to intimidate intruders, the male red-winged blackbird fans his tail and spreads his wings to reveal brilliant red shoulder badges, which are a sign of his age and experience.

duce theirs as needed; generally speaking, the larger the bird, the larger its territory requirements, but factors such as food supply and the population of the habitat also dictate how much space a bird will occupy. A pair of golden eagles may use 90 square kilometres of territory. But the territory of birds that live in colonies and raise their young side by side with those of their neighbours can take up as little space as the nest itself.

After the breeding season, many birds abandon their territories, congregating in flocks for the few weeks before they leave for their winter homes. But a vacant territory can quickly be taken over by a new owner. What was once a well-protected woodpecker cavity may be occupied by chickadees, which will use it as a nightly roost over winter, or by owls, which will make it into a permanent home.

While it is not usually possible to see what a bird's territory really looks like, the male red-winged blackbird regularly patrols the borders of his property. In any roadside marsh, you will see a redwing flying in a systematic pattern from cattail to cattail calling out to declare his ownership. After spending a day watching, you can plot out a map of the redwing's territory and get an idea of the size of the area that each bird covers and the boundaries that he considers to be his own.

A mischievous laughing gull endures the vocal onslaught from a colony of nesting royal terns trying to defend their territory.

Barely visible through the ocean's thick morning haze, thousands of gannets are squeezed onto every available ledge of a rocky cliff. Overcrowding causes many problems in a colony of wild birds; each bird must secure a territory, which creates competition among the residents. There is an air of uneasy truce periodically interrupted by a flurry of jabbing bills. Yet for more than one-eighth of all bird species, living in colonies is a popular strategy.

A colony originates during the breeding season when birds are most competitive, so there is a continual fight for food and nesting sites. The monogamous pairing established by nesting seabirds is constantly at risk because of aggressive males that try to increase the number of their offspring by mating with nearby females. Nesting females are ruthless in their treatment of neighbouring offspring: gulls and terns peck strays to death, while cliff swallows raid adjoining nests to push both eggs and hatchlings out.

Birds such as puffins venture from the colony to forage together, travelling great distances every day in search of food to bring back to their nestlings. Thousands of hungry offspring may strain the available food sources, and as a consequence, many nestlings are small and weak. Young seabirds must be fat when they leave the nest if they are to survive the long delay before they learn to hunt for themselves. A food shortage early on adds stress once they set out.

Nestling birds and their parents

Three white ibises perched preening near their colony.

also feel the impact of parasitic insects. With only centimetres separating the thousands of birds in a large seabird colony, every nest swarms with lice and fleas, many of which rest dormant over the winter, waiting for their hosts to return in the spring. When you consider all the disadvantages, you have to wonder why some birds live in colonies.

Despite the drawbacks, however, life in large, gregarious colonies, like those of puffins, murres and gulls, also offers many advantages. Some naturalists believe that a colony actually serves as an information centre for its members. Birds that travel great distances to their food sources benefit from letting the most successful hunters lead them to the food supply. Because flying insects swarm for only a short period of time, inexperienced cliff and bank swallows will watch for birds that return to the nest with prey and follow them on later trips.

While the abundance of eggs and offspring will always attract pirating

Northern gannet nesting colonies may contain thousands of nests and can spread over hundreds of coastline hectares.

This king penguin rookery is situated beyond the range of land predators yet is conveniently located near a food source. While the colony attracts predators, the hatchlings and eggs are well guarded.

gulls and crows to a colony, a large population provides greater security. Hundreds of pairs of eyes reduce a predator's opportunities to catch a bird by surprise, and when a large number of inhabitants are off hunting, there are always many on guard back at the colony. Cliff and bank swallows warn one another of a possible attack with alarm calls that rally all colony members to mob the predatory bird.

Since breeding birds synchronize the laying of their eggs, predators have few opportunities to rob from the colony. All breeding birds lay their eggs within a relatively short period of time and thereby "swamp" the predators so that they can eat only a small percentage of the young.

The challenge of living cooperatively is something with which most humans can identify, since our cities produce their own mix of advantages and disadvantages. And as in a city, with its crowded, bustling activity, the traffic of birds coming and going and the social squabbles and alliances within a colony make it an exciting place to observe.

A harvest of mountain ash berries is a shared feast for a mixed flock of nomadic Bohemian and cedar waxwings.

Bohemian waxwings are fruit-eaters. A ripe mountain ash tree is precious stock, and when waxwings are nesting, a territory with a rich fruit harvest is well worth a fight. Waxwings, like most birds, are territorial during the breeding season. But as soon as the season is over, waxwings form into flocks.

Once the fighting for exclusive territory ends, birds of the same and mixed species flock together to feed, preen and sleep. Predators are one reason to flock. Flocks intimidate predators such as owls, eagles and hawks because the possibility of capturing one meal is not worth the risk of collision with so many small birds. A wing injury could send a raptor crashing to the ground or leave it unable to hunt. And if a raptor tries to isolate a straggler, a flock of tiny songbirds can suddenly change direction and swarm it.

Normally, a bird foraging alone spends more than half of its time watching for an approaching attacker. But a group of birds has many pairs of eyes looking for danger, and the added protection that a flock guarantees frees up each individual's time. Even flocks of mixed species with a variety of diets can improve their foraging, as one species may indirectly help the others locate food. Seed- and fruiteaters, which are attracted to bushes ripe with vegetation, can inadvertently flush out flies, moths and other insects for the insectivorous birds flying with them.

Some birds flock to feast on a seasonal abundance of food. Prior to their long flight south, migratory birds such as golden plovers and sandpipers will travel hundreds of kilometres off their regular route to gather and devour the last supplies of their favourite insects. Highly territorial bald eagles make a spectacular flock on the West Coast each year in anticipation of a feast of salmon.

On cold nights, flocking birds keep one another warm in the communal roost. Grouped together in the hollow trunk of a tree or huddled closely on a branch, these birds are warmed by the body heat generated by each of their neighbours. In a penguin rookery, the temperature at the centre of the flock can be 10 Celsius degrees higher than it is at the perimeter. Tiny birds such as chickadees and sparrows are able to survive the below-freezing Canadian winters by huddling together in the roost. As the group generates warmth, the extra bodies work like insulation to contain the heat. With less of its own body exposed, each bird is able to reduce the amount of heat it loses.

While birds do flock together, it is not always a trouble-free arrangement. Starlings crowded side by side on a fence rail or a power line will not hesitate to peck an encroaching neighbour, and it is a common sight to see sparrows and pigeons squabbling over food. Every flock is organized according to a hierarchy that is based on size and seniority. Any newcomer is always the first in line for abuse and the last in line for food.

One of the best ways to study flocks is to run a feeder in winter. In no time, it will become apparent that the social life of a flock is a complicated one. Some birds eat the best food and stand on the best perches, while others must be satisfied with pecking at the seeds that fall to the ground. A few, like the grosbeaks, show up erratically. The jays are always around. You will also notice the birds scanning the area for approaching predators, like the neighbourhood cat, or for such competitors as a hungry squirrel that will scramble onto the feeder.

Following the breeding season, starlings forage in enormous flocks during the day and roost together at night.

As early as August, the first flocks of snow geese abandon their Arctic breeding ground and migrate south for the winter.

In September, flocks of snow geese leave their Arctic summer homes and head for the lush Louisiana marshlands that wind along the coast of the Gulf of Mexico. The flocks follow a flyway through the central plains, where the birds feed on grain and corn remnants from the autumn harvest. With a good tailwind, they can make the transcontinental flight in two days.

While we shiver through the first cold snap of autumn, a mass exodus takes place as five billion birds fly southward. When the cold weather hits, it destroys the food supply of most birds and makes it impossible for them to remain on their northern breeding grounds. Instead, they follow the sun south, where there is a fresh supply of food and more daylight hours for foraging.

Migration is a gruelling test for small birds; in a typical year, only half of the songbirds that attempt the journey will return. To survive, the insect-eating songbirds feed continuously during the final weeks before their food supply shuts down for the season. Using the energy-draining flapping flight, most songbirds must carry up to 50 percent additional body weight to sustain themselves on the trip. Seabirds fly a coastal route and are able to replenish their energy stores as they go. Eagles, vultures, storks and herons reduce the demands of the long distance by using their broad-wing soaring techniques, and geese and ducks fly in energy-efficient V formations that reduce wind resistance.

Most North American birds migrate to Mexico and Central America, where they face increasingly fierce competition for food and sometimes for territory. The winter grounds provide only a fraction of the space available in the vast North, and as the tropical forests are cleared, an already overpopulated winter home is being reduced so drastically that it threatens to leave millions of birds homeless. Some biologists now think that returning to the summer breeding territory is, in fact, a relief from the predator pressure and the competition for food which many birds experience while trying to survive in the South.

Although we understand why birds migrate, no one really knows for sure how they navigate during migration. Following migrating birds is difficult, and whatever the instinct is that guides them operates briefly only twice a year. But there are a number of theories. One speculates that birds use a "getting-warmer" approach to finding a winter home, but that does not explain the pinpoint accuracy which leads some birds back to exactly the same tree year after year. Another suggestion is that birds learn the migration route when they fly in flocks headed by more experienced travellers. Landmarks associated with smell, sight and sound become imprinted on the birds' memory and help to guide them on future trips. Experiments have shown that birds use the sun during the day and the stars at night to guide them when they travel, just as we use compasses and maps. But the fact that they can migrate in cloudy weather suggests that birds also use some other direc-

tional system. Another theory is that birds are sensitive to the Earth's magnetic field, which orients them throughout their trip. All of these techniques may in fact operate together.

Whatever the explanation, migration is an extraordinary behaviour that allows birds to make a home in two radically different habitats, usually situated thousands of kilometres apart, and thus ensures their survival. The lonely calls of geese flying overhead on their journey south remind us that if we hope to see birds return each spring, we must make every effort to preserve their distant winter homes.

Uniting along the flyway, snow geese arrive at their Gulf Coast destination in flocks that may number in the thousands.

Overwintering

Perched on a bare tree branch, a mourning dove soaks up the rays of the winter sun and then ruffles its feathers to trap the heat. Birds have a high body temperature, but they quickly lose their heat to the environment; even at the best of times, it is difficult for birds to keep warm. In winter, when food is in short supply and birds are exposed to the cold air and icy winds, life is especially hard. In order to survive, all overwintering birds must minimize their heat loss by both eating enough food to keep their systems energized and sleeping in a warm place at night.

By the time the cold weather arrives, however, most food sources have disappeared or are frozen solid in ice. Insect populations have declined, and the few overwintering survivors have gone into hibernation. Green vegetation and fruit supplies have already fallen from the trees and bushes, and fruit- and insect-eating species are forced to migrate southward to find food.

In anticipation of the cold, many overwintering birds put on extra weight. But there is a limit to how much bulk a bird can store and still be able to fly. While it benefits from having an energy reserve to burn up during the night, a fat bird is more easily caught by predators, and the extra time spent foraging in winter, without the cover of ground vegetation, places the bird at risk.

Several bird species, however,

Almost exclusively a seed-eating bird, the mourning dove survives in its habitat all winter by visiting bird feeders and foraging for seeds from wild grasses and cut grain.

While the white-tailed ptarmigan forages on open land during the winter, its camouflage plumage hides it from predators.

overwinter in the North, and they survive by exploiting the available food resources. Raptors are able to overwinter by feeding on a steady supply of small mammals such as mice, voles and rabbits; in years when the hunting is especially good, owls will breed during the winter months. Many overwintering birds, like waxwings, sparrows and cardinals, are seed-eaters. Seeds, which are rich in oil and carbohydrates, provide an excellent source of winter food. They are available year-round, and if necessary, they store well. Small birds, such as sparrows, chickadees and woodpeckers, survive on seed supplies cached during times of abundance.

Just as humans wear heavy winter coats, many birds survive the cold by growing heavier plumage.

Most overwintering birds carry 50 percent more plumage than they do during the breeding season. But even with the extra plumage, a bird runs the risk of freezing at night. Sparrows and starlings reduce the loss of body heat by taking advantage of shelter provided by humans and building insulated nests under caves and loose boards. Other birds, like grouse and snow buntings, burrow into the ground and dig out an igloo, exploiting the insulating properties of snow.

Chickadees and some woodpeckers roost communally to keep warm. Huddled inside the shell of a dead tree trunk, where they are protected from the winter wind, as many as a hundred chickadees heat up the tree overnight. Unlike bears or groundhogs, birds are too small to

hibernate, but some economize on energy by lowering their metabolic rate and falling into what is known as a torpor.

For a few species that remain in the North year-round, though, winter is less of a hardship than migration would be. In the North, birds are prey to foxes, cats, humans and other birds, but a seasonal migrant in its winter habitat is likewise prey to such tropical hazards as snakes and monkeys.

There are other advantages to staying put for the winter. Year-round residency provides a real opportunity for a species to control a territory. House sparrows have seized many prime nesting areas in the North because, in the absence of other residents, there is nothing to stop them. Along with the common pigeon, or rock dove, house sparrows have ensured their permanent position by breeding successfully during the winter months.

So when the snow comes, don't put your binoculars and notebook away. Birds that remain in the North are highly active. Owls forage by the light of day; grouse patrol the fields and forests; and flocks of chickadees, nuthatches and woodpeckers swarm through the woods. With no obstructing leaves, it is easier to see all this activity.

People look twice when they see a loggerhead shrike. Bluish grey with black streaks around its eyes, wings and tail, it is a delicate-looking bird whose bill resembles that of a falcon—jagged and sharp, with a miniature hook at the tip. But the loggerhead shrike does not turn heads just because of the way it looks. It is known to impale an assortment of mice, frogs, bees, flies, caterpillars and moths on the barbs of a farmer's fence or on a hawthorn shrub. The only truly predatory songbird, the shrike stores its food for safekeeping until ready to feed.

There are as many bird diets and hunting styles as there are birds. Nothing escapes the bird's diet; every plant and animal group on the face of the Earth appears—berries, fruit, seeds, green plants, microorganisms, insects, snakes, fish, mammals and even other birds.

Gram for gram, a bird eats more than any other animal, and for some, that means eating as much as half its body weight daily. A high metabolic rate causes a bird to burn energy faster than any vertebrate other than the shrew. Consequently, foraging for food is one of a bird's most important activities.

While the bill and feet are the essential tools for feeding, each bird has other physical characteristics that help it forage successfully. Loons and waterfowl are strong swimmers, able to hold their breath while swimming more than 200 metres underwater. Birds of prey ease the energy cost of long hours spent hunting by using soaring flight, something they are uniquely

The loggerhead shrike is a carnivorous songbird that hunts beetles, caterpillars, frogs, mice and other songbirds.

adapted to do because they have enormous wings. Owls use their keen senses of smell and hearing to capture mice and voles scurrying beneath the snow.

Each bird has evolved a strategy designed to obtain the greatest amount of food for the least amount of effort. Robins tend to exploit one feeding area at a time, which saves on travel and provides a familiar environment in which to work. Often, a male and female divide their ter-

ritory in half so that they can make sure the entire area is hunted without covering any part of it twice. Another way to economize on foraging is to construct the nest near the feeding grounds. Marsh birds such as red-winged blackbirds eat insects; they are able to collect most of their food near their nest, which they place among tall grasses.

Some birds further economize on hunting time and energy by increasing the yield of each trip. If the nestlings are hungry, it is in the foraging parent's interest to return to the nest with more than a single serving. If the food is abundant and not too awkward to transport, it makes sense to carry several items back to the nest on each trip. Fishing birds, like pelicans, can collect many fish in their stomachs while hunting and then regurgitate them when they return to the nest. Puffins spend a great deal of time travelling to their food source and lots of energy diving for fish; for them, multiple prey loading makes each trip worthwhile. When the puffin has a hungry nestling to feed, it forages for food by diving into the water and filling its bill crosswise with as many as 30 small fish.

But a large prey load is guaranteed to attract the attention of hungry scroungers. A bill filled with food is irresistible to fish pirates like gulls and frigate birds, which intentionally nest near colonies of seabirds, like puffins and terns, in order to rob them of their catches when

Ravens, like their blue jay and crow cousins, are well-known food pirates that steal many of their meals.

The puffin makes each of its foraging trips worthwhile.

they come back from hunting trips.

Frigate birds specialize in midair theft, following and hounding a bird carrying an appealing catch, even plucking at its tail feathers, until it releases its prey. Before the fish hits the water, however, the frigate bird swoops down and snatches it. The chase is all the more worthwhile if several fish are at stake. In a defensive move, many raptors, like falcons, do not travel with their prey but gorge themselves immediately after it is caught, fanning their wings and hunching over the food to shield it from view. Even the little house sparrow steals from robins, pigeons and other sparrows.

Scroungers are not the only birds that do not hunt their own prey. Ravens wait patiently for scraps from fishing grizzly bears. Turkey vultures sniff out and feed on carrion, the decaying carcass of another animal's hunt. But such scavengers are robbed by more aggressive black vultures, which, lacking a sense of smell, use their eyes to spot flocks of feeding turkey vultures to locate their next meal.

Birds do not always compete for food. On occasion, pairs of bald eagles cooperate to chase rabbits, hares and ground squirrels out of the cover of a densely overgrown forest. Pelicans paddle along in large flocks to herd schools of fish into shallow bays, where they can easily use their huge dip-net bills to scoop up many fish at a time.

When it comes to handling their prey, birds that eat seeds have an easier time than birds that feed on insects or mammals. Seed collection

A screech owl approaches in silence, aided by the specially designed sawtooth tip on the forward edge of each flight feather, which deadens the sound of air whispering through its wings.

is a low-risk method of foraging that requires little effort; relatively easy to obtain in a good territory, seeds are also a high-energy form of food that stores well. Most seed-eaters can cache, or store, seeds for use during seasons when food is not abundant, and most species that overwinter are seed-eating birds which rely on caches of nuts they have scattered throughout their territory as insurance against thievery.

The cycle of food abundance eventually affects seed-eaters as well. In seasons of low yield, every seed is devoured by some kind of animal, and the resulting food shortage causes a decline in bird populations through starvation or poor reproduction. The reduced bird population allows seed crops to flourish once again; after a couple of years, an abundance of seeds leads to a bird population explosion. The risk of food shortages means that exclusively seed-eating birds such as crossbills are highly migratory and have adapted to breed any month of the year to take advantage of what may be a short-lived food supply.

We are just beginning to appreciate the foraging abilities of birds. For years, birders have wondered how the robin finds worms, and for a long time, it was assumed that they hunted simply by sight. Scientists have discovered, however, that robins also hunt using their hearing. When a robin hops across the lawn, stopping to cock its head to one side, it is listening for the sound of worms crawling through the soil. For bird watchers, even the common robin is full of surprises.

With a firm grip on its prey, an American robin throws its whole body into pulling a juicy earthworm from the ground.

Many fruit-eating birds, like the robin, are attracted to the ripe berries of the mountain ash tree and readily disperse its seeds.

In early spring, berries are hard, green and sour, and they can sit undisturbed on the branches of trees and bushes for months. But with the hot, sunny days of summer, the berries ripen and hang from the branches fleshy, brightly coloured and irresistible. While the luscious clusters of fruit are easy targets for caterpillars, worms and other insects, one of the ways the plant survives is by attracting fruit-eating birds.

The success of a plant often rests with getting its seeds spread over as wide an area as possible. Some seeds, like those of the milkweed, are light and feathery and float great distances before landing. Others, such as maple keys, are designed to twirl away from the parent plant on a gust of wind. But many seeds, like cherries, are big, heavy and bound up in a fruit covering, so they do not fall far from the tree. Since birds not only like to eat fruit but also travel long distances, they are excellent dispersers of these sorts of seeds.

To ensure the maximum distribution of its seeds, a plant must attract the courier as often as possible. While collecting fruit is not the most exhausting form of hunting, fruit has no protein. The sugary pulp is burned up quickly by the bird's system, and the bird must return frequently to the tree to feed. The more often it returns, the better it is for the plant.

Fruit-eating birds do not have teeth with which to chew, but they have specially adapted bills and throat muscles that allow them to swallow the food whole. The

A specially adapted long, curved bill allows the Clark's nutcracker to remove seeds from between the scales of a cone.

pulp is quickly digested, and the seeds are regurgitated or passed from the body intact. Some birds do not even swallow the larger seeds; they simply clean off the flesh, then drop the pit onto the ground. Some pits, like those of the cherry, are discouragingly tough, which makes them almost impossible — and sometimes dangerous — for the bird to swallow.

Not all seed dispersal is the result of fruit eating. Many birds distribute seeds by hiding them in the ground. Since seeds store well, caching contributes to their dispersal. The Clark's nutcracker is the sole disperser of the high-fat seed of the whitebark pine. Unlike most cones, those of the whitebark pine are tightly scaled and must be forced open so that the heavy, flat seeds can be removed. Only the Clark's nutcracker has the long, curved bill necessary to pry the scales apart. By scatter-storing thousands of seeds in ground caches throughout its territory, the nutcracker plants many whitebark pine trees.

Most plants do not rely exclusively on the efforts of birds to distribute their seeds, because not all seed- and fruit-eating birds are good dispersers. A seed that is ground into a gritty pulp does not stand much of a chance of becoming a plant, and although many grazing birds like turkeys and grouse eat fruit, the gravelly gizzard that enables them to digest tough vegetation destroys most seeds. Other nuts are just too big for birds. The acorn woodpecker, for example, is the only bird that can eat chestnuts and acorns. Since it wedges the seeds into the bark crevices of a tree trunk, however, the seeds are not dispersed until the cache is raided by squirrels, which take away the nuts to stash in the ground, where many eventually grow into trees.

Like any living organism, birds will feast on the abundance of food available in a fruit orchard full of unprotected trees, and as a result, birds are often viewed as an enemy of agriculture. Yet when we look at the trees around us — oak, wild cherry and mountain ash — it is clear that long before humans farmed the land, birds were responsible for planting many of the orchards and old forests upon which we all rely.

Habitat

Ducks and water have gone together for thousands of years. The lives of ducks revolve around water: they swim, feed and breed near water. When ducklings hatch, their first excursion is to the safety of a nearby pond.

What a bird considers adequate for living is known as its habitat. Most birds are suited for specific habitats, such as densely overgrown woods, the forest edge, mountainous seaside cliffs, the Arctic, swamps and marshes, cities, sandy beaches, lush tropical forests and deserts. Over the course of its natural history, each species has survived by using behaviours that increase its opportunities to feed and to nest safely in its habitat and so will return to familiar surroundings when it is time to breed.

Birds that have a general diet and flexible nesting habits are broadly adapted and can live in a variety of areas. There is one thing they all share: a bird's habitat must contain both nest sites and the type of food the bird eats. Cliff swallows inhabit open, elevated areas, such as rocky cliff faces, where they construct adherent nests. Because they are open-air foragers—consuming insects that they catch in flight—they position themselves where they feed. Ospreys are found almost everywhere there is water. From the Far North to the Tropics, ospreys inhabit lakes, marshes, rivers, ocean

This green-winged teal and her offspring need their aquatic habitat. Ducks are adapted as swimming birds, nesting near water and feeding on the plants that grow in freshwater ponds.

shores and mangrove swamps. Wherever there are fish to catch and trees or cliffs to nest on, ospreys will make their home.

Marsh birds enjoy both an abundance of food and the cover of tall marsh reeds to protect them, but no habitat is perfect. The marsh is equally attractive to many other species that are a threat to nesting birds. Muskrats, snakes and even bullfrogs devour the eggs and the young of most marsh species.

Occasionally, birds move out of their regular habitat. Turkey vultures, which feed on the carcasses of freshly killed or decomposing animals, have recently begun living in populated areas. Under normal circumstances, vultures find their food and choose their territory by shadowing populations of such large carnivores as wolves and wildcats. But their move has probably been influenced by the availability of road-killed animals from busy highways. The move has not affected their nesting success, since turkey vultures simply lay their eggs on bare ground or in vegetation.

Likewise, it is not unusual to see a cliff swallow's mud-plastered nest on the eaves of a downtown office tower. In a city, cliff swallows do not face the same predator pressure from gulls and terns that they do in their natural habitat. But the transition is not without drawbacks; the construction of skyscrapers has cost the lives of thousands of night-feeding birds, which perish when they smash into darkened office windows in their search for food.

Only a few bird species can sur-

Facing hardship in an ever-shrinking wilderness, the peregrine falcon has been introduced into large urban centres.

vive in disturbed environments. Some have been able to adapt their nest-building style to conform to human constructions that imitate their natural habitats. Cavity nesters find refuge in the peaks of barn roofs or under loose boards on eave troughs, and if their diet is varied and food is readily available, the transition to an area inhabited by humans can be beneficial.

The robin is a ground-feeding species that has profited from the de-

struction of forests. Every one of its enemies, except the domestic cat, has been destroyed or eliminated by the clearing of forests to make room for cities; as long as there are worms to hunt, the robin will prosper.

The diet and nesting habits of the sparrow are general enough that it can adapt to almost any environment, and because the sparrow overwinters in the North, it has a territorial advantage. A gregarious bird, the house sparrow has managed to intimidate and even out-number many resident species.

The peregrine falcon, nearly eliminated from its natural habitat by DDT poisoning, has been introduced into large cities to live on office towers and feed on pigeons. Skyscrapers resemble the wild, rocky cliffs that are the peregrine's traditional setting. Nests are fashioned from the litter and trash that the peregrine finds on the streets and heaps together on ledges.

Despite the ability of some bird species to adapt to new habitats, however, many birds simply cannot flourish when they are unshielded from the disrupting influence of humans. All birds that need wetlands or forests for nesting are at the greatest risk from habitat loss, since these environments cannot be improvised. Tied to their original territories by their breeding and feeding habits, such species have little hope of adapting to a new type of habitat. Two-thirds of all North American ducks breed in prairie potholes; but since potholes are being ploughed over and drained for agriculture, the ducks are losing their only nesting areas. Loons are water birds that swim to shore to nest but cannot walk on land; they therefore rely on shoreline and small islands. Bluebirds and woodpeckers nest in the decaying stumps of trees and depend on wood-boring insects that are attracted to old timber, while herons and raptors need a habitat with tall, strong trees to support their platform nests.

As forests are clear-cut in order to build cities and as we pollute the

A lush, tropical Costa Rican cloud forest is home to billions of birds, yet it is being destroyed to make room for cash crops.

waterways and eliminate other organisms that live in an ecologically cooperative relationship with them, birds face additional pressures. Farms are no substitute for forests, and shopping malls do not support waterfowl. If a species is to reproduce successfully, it must be allowed to exploit the opportunities of its habitat. Before the countryside is swallowed up by suburbia, we should remind ourselves that as we destroy thousands of hectares of bird-breeding habitat, we move ever closer to a world which can support only pigeons, starlings and garbage-eating gulls.

The coastal home of a colony of northern gannets provides easy access to the ocean. At 3 months, the young birds swim out to sea, where they wait for the final month to pass until they can fly.

Approached by a stalking skunk, a brooding Canada goose accepts the challenge. Rising to its feet, the goose fans its huge wings, throws its chest forward and lets out a harsh honk that proves it means business. The goose has strong wings with a bony edge, and it can deliver a powerful blow to an attacker. Its agitated response has evolved over millions of years as a reaction to constant predator pressure.

There is a long list of animals —badgers, muskrats, wood rats, squirrels, snakes and even turtles— that will make a quick meal of unattended eggs or a family of helpless nestlings. Almost all birds are the target of predation during the early stages of life. Predation pressure on eggs and nestlings is reflected not only in the choice of inaccessible nest sites but in the number of eggs laid. Young ground nesters such as wild turkeys, killdeer and woodcocks are especially vulnerable to attack from carnivores. These birds compensate for their high death rate by raising broods of as many as 15 offspring. For most other species, an out-of-the-way nest is the best defence against attack.

Once a bird is old enough to leave the nest, its chances for survival improve. Most adult birds can fly, making them more elusive targets than a helpless nestling. The larger the bird, the fewer predators it has and the longer its life span. Many

A ground nest is often preyed upon by small mammals. But the Canada goose pair stays together through the breeding season, so there is always a guard ready to chase away an intruder.

small birds survive only a few years in the wild, but some banded birds have been found alive at 12 years of age. Raptors can live to be more than 50, but seabirds, which have relatively little exposure to natural enemies, hold the record for old age. One wandering albatross is thought to have lived past the age of 60.

It can take many small birds to satisfy the appetite of an animal trying to survive on such a diet, and birds are agile, difficult prey, so few species can afford to specialize as bird predators. Raptors are the greatest enemies of other birds. Flight gives eagles, hawks, owls and falcons an advantage over most other carnivores when it comes to catching a bird, so many raptors, like owls, will prey on other birds and their offspring when the rodent population is low. Those attacks depend on surprise – usually a high-speed dive from above. That is why raptors spend so much time soaring. In fact, you will notice whenever songbirds see a raptor over-

A hungry badger on the prowl finds a high-protein feast at an unattended nest of mallard eggs.

head, they dive for cover in alarm.

Humans pose a different and much more dramatic threat to birds than do animals or other birds. The incredible pressure that hunting exerts on bird populations is well documented. In the last century, the sky was black with flocks of passenger pigeons that lived wild throughout North America. But during the late 1800s, tens of thousands were killed daily until they were all eliminated. In Italy, the entire songbird population has been virtually wiped out to satisfy gourmet appetites; and in Japan, supple, smooth penguin hides are in demand for the production of expensive gloves. Every year, North American eagles die in baited leghold traps that hunters do not bother to check.

Natural mortality and predation place enough pressure on bird populations without the added menace of individual human interference. Naturalists should be aware of their own impact on the world of birds. Every time we tear down an inhabited nest that has been constructed under an eave trough, we threaten bird populations. Rather than destroying a constructed nest, take the time after the breeding season to repair any holes under eave troughs and to block loose boards with chicken wire. If gently discouraged, birds will choose other nest sites.

Conservationist-banded ducks downed by hunters.

Birds as Predators

During the winter, a great grey owl perches on the lowest branch of a bare tree, studies the ground and waits. Without making a sound, the owl slips from the tree and glides on fully spread wings – floating to earth as silently as a falling leaf – to scoop up a scurrying vole. Some years, the hunting is this easy all season long.

Humans have not always understood the role birds play in controlling small-animal populations. Some small-bird species, like open-air for-aging martins, swifts and swallows, consume thousands of insects every day – mosquitoes, midges, flies and moths – that if left unchecked could not only damage crops but also make this planet unbearably buggy for humans. Today, farmers appreciate the value of insect-eating birds; some even use flocks of geese rather than chemicals to reduce the otherwise uncontrollable populations of flies in the barnyard.

In fact, true predatory birds such as hawks, eagles and owls were once the target of attack by humans. We believed that raptors threatened the survival of small mammals. But birds of prey hunt gophers that dig treacherous tunnels through fields, ground squirrels that graze on vegetation, and magpies and crows that damage crops and harass injured farm animals. When the populations of small animals do fluctuate, factors other than the feeding habits of raptors are responsible.

During years when there is a good crop of buds, berries, seeds, grasses and insects, the populations of such prey animals as mice, voles, rabbits and grouse explode. These are feast years for birds of prey, a time when breeding pairs rear many chicks. Even during the feast, prey species can still reproduce faster than the raptors are able to eat them.

But eventually, the populations of prey animals collapse from disease caused by overcrowding and from starvation brought on by a strained food supply. This means famine for the raptors. Most birds cannot breed during years of food shortage and, to survive, must migrate long distances outside their normal range to find a new food supply. The great grey and snowy owls are periodic winter nomads that travel south from their northern habitat to track food.

Fortunately, birds of prey are long-lived, so sporadic reproduction does not jeopardize their overall success; they have many more years in their lifetime to produce offspring. But raptors do face a more deadly threat. Their diet often exposes them to the chemicals that hu-

In some years, a great grey owl enjoys lots of vole meals, but the prey species' population cycle can create a famine.

mans use in agriculture and industry. As a result, raptors have become an important measure of the human abuse of the environment.

Once an agricultural or industrial toxin enters the environment — whether it is dumped directly into our lakes and rivers or washes in through the soil — it enters the food chain and eventually turns up in the raptor's diet — in salmon contaminated with mercury or DDT, in a ground squirrel that has eaten vegetation sprayed with insecticide or in a duck full of lead shot or strychnine-laced grain that was put out to poison a gopher.

An insecticide such as DDT has a devastating effect on the reproduction of a bird like the osprey or the bald eagle. Sometimes, DDT contamination causes infertility; other times, it weakens the eggshell so that the weight of a bird cracks it during incubation. When the populations of raptors are affected by such contamination, it signals a general deterioration of the environment. While the use of DDT is now restricted, we must continue to pay attention to the state of birds; their health is a reflection of our own.

Adept at capturing insects in flight, the eastern bluebird helps control insect populations throughout the North.

Every year, millions of birds are the innocent victims of humans. The plastic six-pack holders that are carelessly discarded from boats are death traps for waterfowl. Entangled in the synthetic noose, a bird is unable to swallow and slowly chokes or starves to death.

At the same pace that we strip our planet of its resources, we casually toss our industrial and residential waste back at nature, dumping it into rivers and adding to already overflowing solid-waste dump sites. And wildlife populations have been dramatically affected: herring gulls have abandoned shoreline habitats because they have greater success feeding in dumps; whales are poisoned by industrial pollutants seeping into our waterways; sea turtles and porpoises choke to death on plastic bags that they mistake for jellyfish; and seabirds die from diets of oil-contaminated fish.

Other dangers that face the natural world are created by industry and supported by government. Fishing trollers in search of their daily quotas are permitted to sweep international waters with huge plastic drift nets. But these "walls of death" inevitably trap thousands of seabirds – puffins, gulls, albatrosses and terns – and large marine mammals. The short-term gain of a big catch is eventually paid for by the long-term threat to wildlife.

Each year, hunters fire thousands

Because of the careless disposal of nonbiodegradable materials by humans, this Canada goose has become ensnared in a plastic noose. The bird will starve to death because it is unable to swallow.

of lead shotgun pellets that settle to the bottom of ponds, where they are mistaken for seeds and eaten by bottom-feeding waterfowl like ducks, geese and swans. It takes only two or three pellets to affect a bird, and a bird poisoned by lead experiences a slow and torturous death. At the outset, it stops eating because its gizzard is paralyzed; then, suffering from diarrhea and furiously vomiting the bile that its gallbladder will not stop secreting, the bird becomes weak, its muscles deteriorate, and it is unable to fly. For days, it flops around helplessly, and when it eventually dies from starvation, it is only half its previous body weight. It has been more than a hundred years since the first avian casualties of lead poisoning were discovered, and yet to this day, there is no law in Canada that requires the use of nontoxic ammunition.

Every time a forest is cleared, it takes centuries to replace what is lost. Our consumption of cheap, disposable products affects the rate at which mature forests are cut down. The need for new materials and the destruction of habitats can be arrested only through an organized recycling programme: we need to protect more land against development that causes habitat destruction. Currently, a mere 2.6 percent of the uninhabited land in Canada is protected as wilderness. Only 6.3 percent has any kind of protected status at all. This is far too little. Even the most conservative estimate recommends that at least 12 percent of any country should be protected habitat.

Great, cattle and snowy egrets, white ibises, crows and gulls evicted from their habitats thrive in an overflowing dump.

When hunting pressure is added to habitat destruction, the ultimate consequence is species extinction. The situation is worsening. Twelve more North American bird species were recently added to the endangered species list.

Yet because human behaviour is at the root of the problems, solutions are not impossible. In the late 1960s, the eastern bluebird was on the verge of extinction. An overwintering species, bluebirds traditionally nested in tree stumps and woodpecker holes and fed on the host of insects attracted to the old timber. As stands of timber were cleared for development, however, bluebird populations had to discover new habitats. Some migrated to the countryside and nested in wooden fenceposts, but as farms modernized and concrete and steel replaced wood, many died, unable to adapt yet another time. Recognizing the threat, conservationists developed a programme that provided bluebirds with nest boxes in which they could raise their young. The bluebird population is now on the rise.

Humans can aid bird life directly – by taking action such as the bluebird recovery programme – and together, we can work for a society that reduces levels of waste and pollution and, ideally, produces fewer humans. As long as our populations continue to grow, there will be less room for wildlife.

If you have seen a compact, mostly grey little bird with a black cap and throat, a white cheek and light underside—a bird small enough to cradle in your hand—you have seen the black-capped chickadee, one of the most recognizable birds in North America. Not all birds are as easy to identify; it can take years to tell the many warblers apart. Identifying a bird is like solving a mystery. The only difference is that you do not have to go looking for clues; nearly everything you need to know is right in front of your eyes.

One of the pleasures of bird watching is that it does not require special equipment. Binoculars, if you have a pair, can be helpful for giving you a close-up look at your subject, but your eyes, ears and curious mind are your most important tools. To confirm your observations, you will need a good field guide, one that contains a description and a picture of all the birds found in your region, and you will also want to have a notebook and a pencil to record your observations.

Like any other sport, birding is competitive. The family of birds is so extensive that some people spend a lifetime travelling around the world trying to see them all. Their pride and joy is the list they keep, almost like a scoreboard, of bird sightings—many common, some unusual and some rare. While identification is rewarding, it is only the first step in bird study. After identifying your subject, you can go on to the more elaborate study of birds and their behaviours.

Bird identification is a step-by-step process of elimination that begins with determining where your subject lives, its range and its habitat. One of the most important clues in identifying a bird is its geographic range, so before you leave home, personalize your field guide with bookmarks or colours to highlight the birds that inhabit your observation area. Because a bird's specific habitat choice could be important information when you are making the identification, pay close attention to whether you see the bird on a lake, in a marsh, in a coniferous tree or in an open field.

Since sunlight and shadows misrepresent the colours of feathers, the size and shape of the bird's body are your next clues. Different birds have distinctive body shapes and features. Learn to distinguish the silhouette of a raptor such as an owl, an eagle or a hawk from that of a songbird or a duck. Also, look carefully at the shapes of the bill, feet, tail

Showing little fear of humans, the black-capped chickadee is easily encouraged to land on a hand offering seeds.

and wings in flight. Certain features provide unmistakable hints about the bird's identity – a hooked bill, for instance, belongs to a raptor, while webbed feet are characteristic of a water bird. But a sighting may happen quickly. If you do not have the time to look up the bird's identity while you are in the wild, draw the shape and describe its features in your notebook, and wait until you get home to look in a field guide.

Each bird species has distinctive markings – such as the colour of its legs, a throat patch, a bar of colour on the wings – that set it apart from other species. These key features are known as field marks. While they are sometimes difficult to see at a distance, such features will enable you to pin down the precise species and sex of the bird. Binoculars will help you to determine whether the red appears on the bird's shoulder or tail, and that information will tell you whether you have spotted a red-shouldered or a red-tailed hawk.

Keeping records can be one of the most satisfying aspects of bird watching. Your notes describing the bird, the date of the sighting and any of its behaviours, such as the location and size of its nest or the number of eggs, will give you something to share with fellow birders. In years to come, you will have a record that will remind you of fine days spent getting to know a new bird.

The calliope hummingbird is attracted to the colour red and therefore can be lured to a feeder displaying a red spout.

Wildlife photographer Bruce Lyon will do almost anything to take a picture, but it is not the camera that sends him over the edge of Baffin Island's rocky coast, dangling from a rope. Lyon is a biologist, and his daredevil adventures are all part of his work – studying birds. Fortunately, bird study is not always quite so dangerous. If you can satisfy some of their basic needs – food, water and shelter – you can work with birds in your own backyard.

Backyard bird watching is one of the easiest ways to learn how some birds live. You can observe how birds communicate, their feeding habits and, if you are lucky, nest building and parental care during the breeding season. The experience and information you gain by starting close to home will give you a head start once you get out into the field.

Winter is a great time of year to start attracting birds to your yard. Because overwintering species have a difficult time finding food, most are willing to come out into the open to get a free meal. Once you start putting out food, you may draw more than the usual population to your area. Despite their appreciation of a new food source, however, many birds are selective eaters. To attract them to your yard, the food must be fresh, and you must offer a food for each type of diet – seed, insect and fruit.

Sunflower seeds will attract most birds to your yard and are especially popular among chickadees, cardinals, blue jays and sparrows, which prefer to eat from a feeder. But

Biologist Bruce Lyon surveys a colony of thick-billed murres to compare their diet with their rate of growth.

many other seed-eating birds, like pigeons, are ground feeders, and while they will eat sunflower seeds, they prefer crushed seeds, such as millet, hemp, rice and scratch corn, spread near bushes and shrubs. They can then peck at small bits of food while under cover. Experiment with a variety of seeds and nuts.

During the coldest months of the year, overwintering chickadees, nuthatches, creepers and wood-

peckers love to eat suet and peanut butter. It is impossible for these birds to find a high-protein diet to substitute for insects in winter, and the fat content of such food gives them the necessary nourishment to survive. Spread it onto the trunk of a tree so that the birds can feed naturally, plucking small pieces of food from the crevices of the bark.

Fruit-eaters such as waxwings and bluebirds will welcome raisins and dried currants or apples. If you have fruit-bearing trees or bushes nearby, cut the stalks with excess berries at the end of the growing season and dry them to feed to the birds during winter. (If the berries are not eaten within a few days, clean them out of the feeder because they can ferment in wet weather and do the birds more harm than good.)

With such a variety of food preferences and feeding styles, it is inevitable that there will be competition around the feeder in winter. Large birds will dominate and chase away smaller birds, many of which are unaccustomed to feeding on the ground. To keep the different kinds of food separate, arrange as many feeders as possible throughout your yard. Remember that tree squirrels can climb up a pole or down a rope to get at a feeder. If you want to prevent squirrels from terrorizing the birds, you can do two things: establish a separate feeding station with food that appeals to squirrels to reduce their interest in the bird feed; and place a squirrel guard on the bird feeder to limit their access.

While birds have a high body temperature and lose less moisture to the air than mammals do, they need water year-round – to drink, to bathe in and to feed their young. Trapped in the heat of a dry summer without puddles or water-drenched leaves from which to drink, city-dwelling birds can become dehydrated. In winter, their bodies are under tremendous strain because they are forced to use snow as a source of moisture. To help, you can provide fresh water in the yard. Whether it is used during winter or

Amateur naturalists can become banders and help tag birds as a means of monitoring their behaviour throughout their lives.

summer, a birdbath should never contain more than a few centimetres of water, must be made from a nonmetallic material and should be placed in an elevated spot in the sunlight.

If you construct birdhouses for your backyard, you can help overwintering cavity nesters, like bluebirds, chickadees, woodpeckers and wrens, survive the harshest weather of the year. Be sure you construct the minimum size of entranceway necessary for each type of bird that will use the house. Otherwise, you will find larger and more aggressive species invading the box and removing nesting materials and even eggs. Also, some birds will not use cluttered nest boxes, so when possible, construct birdhouses with removable roofs

that will allow you to clean them between seasons. As with diet, birds have very specific housing preferences. Consult one of the many resource books available to find the design and dimensions that suit the birds which live in your area.

The highlight of bird watching is the breeding season, and by spring, your hard work over the winter may be rewarded by some permanent resident birds nesting in your yard. To encourage them to stay, leave their favourite nesting materials around the yard – straw, short pieces of thread, yarn, bits of fabric and even the hair brushed from your dog or cat – and you might see one weaving the materials into its nest. A family of birds will provide weeks of fascinating entertainment.

CREDITS

4 Courtesy Department of Library Services, American Museum of Natural History
5 Bruce Lyon
6 Kathy Watkins
7 James M. Richards
8 Jerry L. Ferrara
9 Bruce Lyon
10 Mike Pirnke
11 Stephen J. Krasemann, Valan
12 Tim Fitzharris
13 Bruce Lyon
14 Stephen J. Krasemann, DRK Photo
15 Kevin Schafer, Tom Stack & Associates
16 Brian Milne, First Light
17 (top) Dennis W. Schmidt, Valan
17 (bottom) Bruce Lyon
18 Tim Fitzharris
19 David Cavagnaro
20 Bruce Lyon
21 Larry R. Ditto, Bruce Coleman, Inc.
22 Andrius Valadka
23 Wayne Wegner, First Light
24 Frans Lanting, Minden Pictures
25 Robert Villani
26 Robert C. Simpson, Tom Stack & Associates
27 Tim Fitzharris
28 Jen and Des Bartlett, Bruce Coleman, Inc.
29 Bruce Lyon
30 Don and Esther Phillips, Tom Stack & Associates
31 Jerg Kroener
32 Erwin and Peggy Bauer
33 Wayne Lankinen
34 Zig Leszczynski, Animals Animals
35 Tim Fitzharris
36 Frans Lanting, Minden Pictures
37 (top) Mike Blair
37 (bottom) Terry G. Murphy
38 Joseph Van Wormer, Bruce Coleman, Inc.

39 Skylar Hansen
40 Bruce Lyon
41 Bruce Lyon
42 (top) Chuck Gordon
42 (bottom) Tim Fitzharris
43 Wolfgang Kaehler
44 Tom Mangelsen
45 James R. Page
46 Jeff Foott
47 Jerry L. Ferrara
48 Robert McCaw
49 Jeff Foott
50 Robert C. Simpson, Valan
51 (top) Tim Fitzharris
51 (bottom) K. Ghani, Valan
52 James R. Fisher
53 James R. Page
54 Tim Fitzharris
55 Don Johnston, Photo/Nats
56 Harry Engels, Animals Animals
57 Robert Galbraith, Valan
58 Bruce Lyon
59 Tim Fitzharris
60 Thomas Kitchin, Valan
61 (top) Michael S. Quinton
61 (bottom) Stephen J. Krasemann, Valan
62 Michel Julien, Valan
63 Gregory K. Scott, Photo Researchers, Inc.
64 Joe Branney, Tom Stack & Associates
65 Robert Villani
66 Robert P. Carr, Bruce Coleman, Inc.
67 Tom Mangelsen
68 Bruce Lyon
69 Robert C. Simpson, Valan

FURTHER READING

IDENTIFICATION

A Field Guide to the Birds
Roger Tory Peterson
Houghton Mifflin Co., Boston, 1934

Birds of Ontario
J. Murray Speirs
Natural Heritage/Natural History Inc.,
Toronto, 1985

REFERENCE

Audubon Society Encyclopedia of North
     American Birds
John K. Terres
Alfred A. Knopf, New York, 1980

A Dictionary of Birds
Edited by B. Campbell and E. Lack
Buteo Books, South Dakota, 1985

BEHAVIOUR

The Architecture of Animals
Adrian Forsyth
Camden House Publishing, 1989

The Nature of Birds
Adrian Forsyth
Camden House Publishing, 1988

Bird Behaviour
Robert Burton
Consultant Editor Dr. Bruce Campbell
Granada Publishing, London, 1985

A Guide to the Behavior of Common Birds
D.W. Stokes
Little Brown, Boston, 1979

INDEX